OUR
PASSOVER

CHRIST
OUR
PASSOVER

Meditations on the
Mystery of Salvation

STEPHEN REYNOLDS

ABC Publishing
ANGLICAN BOOK CENTRE

ABC Publishing
Anglican Book Centre
600 Jarvis Street
Toronto, Ontario M4Y 2J6

Agnus Dei stained glass window illustration courtesy of All Saints' Anglican Church, Whitby, Ontario: To the Glory of God and in loving memory of Stuart Threadgold and his wife, Alice Speller.

Stained glass window by Robert McCausland Limited, Toronto, Ontario.
Text typeset in Janson
Cover and text design by Jane Thornton
Printed in Canada

National Library of Canada Cataloguing in Publication

Reynolds, Stephen James, 1951-
        Christ our Passover : meditations on the mystery of salvation / Stephen Reynolds.

ISBN 1-55126-385-8

1. Lent—Meditations. 2. Easter—Meditations. I. Title.

BV85.R49 2003   242'.34   C2002-905725-6

Contents

PREFACE

This book does not presume to guide and shepherd you, Christian reader, through the seasons of Lent, Holy Week, and Easter. Instead, it seeks to be one of your companions during your passage from Ash Wednesday to Pentecost and Trinity Sunday; a companion that may give you some food for thought, in the form of meditations on the mystery of salvation. These meditations are based on the proper readings for Sundays and "privileged ferias" in Lent and Eastertide, as appointed in the Revised Common Lectionary.

Some Anglicans may still be a bit uncertain what to think about meditation. It used to occupy the same space in their religious imaginations as, thirty years ago, extra-virgin olive oil occupied in Anglo-Canadian kitchens — something exotic that immigrants cooked with, while they themselves were content to use the vegetable oil of petitionary prayer in private and the butter of Bible-study groups in the parish. Meditation smelt of mystics and spiritual masters, and certain kinds of Anglicanism have always regarded mysticism with squinty-eyed suspicion, either as smacking of irrational "enthusiasm" or, because Jesus said nothing about it in the gospels, as contrary to the Christian message. But times have changed or, at least, are changing. As Anglo-Canadians have discovered that southern European, Middle Eastern, Indian, Chinese, and Japanese cuisines can taste very good indeed, so Anglicans have discovered that there is more to spirituality than taking shopping-lists to the Lord in petitionary prayer. And so the discipline of meditation, so ancient and so new, has gained ever-widening appeal.

But what *is* meditation? In the Christian tradition, it is not a form of navel-gazing that feeds on the private self and its sensitivities alone. Rather, it focuses on the word of God as attested in the holy Scriptures and (as occasion permits or encourages) in the writings of the Christian tradition's teachers of the faith, who were themselves meditating on God's word. What distinguishes this activity from, say, biblical exegesis or ordinary theological discourse is that you employ the text or texts that you are pondering, not to elucidate the thought of the scriptural author or the mind of the Church, so much as to elucidate your relationship with the living God — to hear God more genuinely, to engage God more closely, to respond to God more gladly. In the process, you "unpack" what you are hearing by way of reminiscence and association. The text that your spirit is holding, revolving, even caressing, prompts you to remember other texts from the Scriptures (and other writings in the Christian tradition) that resonate with allied meaning. Meditation, then, is the sort of thinking that develops a network of associations, rather than the sort of thinking that pursues a single line of argument. It mulls on a text in such a way as to let other texts resonate through the first text and link up with it, until a whole web of meaning has emerged. This meaning is in not the mere accumulation of associations but in their connection back to the text that occasioned the train of alliances. Douglas Hofstadter has called these alliances and associations "strange loops" — a process that "by moving upwards (or downwards) through the levels of some hierarchical system, we unexpectedly find ourselves right back where we started." Hofstadter used J. S. Bach's music, M. C. Escher's art, and Kurt Gödel's mathematics to elaborate this motif. As it happens, his description applies equally well to the kind of thinking involved in Christian meditation. It is the kind of thinking known as *lectio divina* ("divine reading"), as practised in the Benedictine tradition of monasticism and its offshoots. At the heart of this meditational discipline is a Christ-centred rumination upon the Scriptures, especially the Psalms, under the guidance of the ancient (and, it may be, mediaeval, seventeenth-century, modern, and contemporary) teachers of the faith.

There are other Christian ways of practising meditation, such as those developed by Ignatius of Loyola (the "Ignatian" method) and by Francis de Sales (the "Salesian" method). But all have this trait in common: they are based on the Scriptures, and seek to be responsible to the word of God for the sake of richer participation in the life of God the Word made flesh, Jesus Christ, "who was handed over to death for our trespasses and was raised for our justification" (Romans 4:25). This, as it happens, is what makes the act of meditating not only a matter of spirituality but also a practice of theology, from the Greek words *theos*, "God," and *logos*, "word." Meditation involves theology insofar as it involves pondering the word of God in order to be open to God in Christ, the Word made flesh — and to continue pondering God's word in the presence of Jesus the incarnate Word, once crucified, now risen and glorified, under the guidance of the Spirit.

This account of meditation, I confess, and will not deny, has a certain amount of self-interest in it. I am a professor of systematic theology in the Faculty of Divinity of Trinity College, Toronto; and, as a priest, I am the Theologian in Residence at the Church of the Redeemer, Toronto. Theology is at once my profession and my pleasure. But I realize that very few Christians, even among those who are training for ordained ministry, share my sense of theology's glad necessity. The very thought of doing theology may give you, Christian reader, the same sort of panic attack you felt before taking the final exam for Grade 12 physics. For that reason, theologians, being practitioners of theology, may cause you to think dark thoughts of the guillotine and the virtues of capital punishment. This isn't to say that theologians are all aristos and you are as Madame Dufarge. Rather, you regard yourself as a decent, church-attending, law-abiding person, and theologians as a sort of biker-gang in tweeds and turtlenecks. If it's "Lock up your daughters!" when bikers show up, it's "Lock up your faith!" when a theologian appears on the scene.

I will admit that, as a class, professional theologians tend to work in a guild-like atmosphere; and, as with most guilds, we tend to be protective of our craft's "mysteries" — its standards of appraisal, its jargon, even its in-jokes. ("How many angels can dance on the head of a pin?" is one of the earliest in-jokes ever recorded; but, precisely because it was an in-joke, everybody else since then has taken it as a question seriously disputed in mediaeval schools of theology.) It needs to be said, however, that the unfriendly attitude of church-people and the general public toward the study of theology and theologians as a class is not altogether fair. For almost eight hundred years, the Church and its theologians have been locked in a relationship that bears all the signs of co-dependency. The Church entrusted its teachings — and the task of teaching its teachings — to the "experts," and all but relinquished education, the ongoing formation of Christian minds, as a dimension of pastoral care for adults as well as children. Having thus made Esau's deal with Jacob, pastors have spent the intervening centuries complaining that the theologians have been behaving like ... well, experts. What is wrong with this picture?

It is no use denying that the study of theology has become a very specialized and arcane field, rather like the upper reaches of quantum physics. It is none of my task here to explore and perhaps explain how this state of affairs came about; but I will say, as a practising theologian, that it ought *not* to have come about. Theology is, or ought to be, the possession and practice of the whole Church; and I would argue that, in fact, what we have is really a two-tiered practice of theology — theology as it is done in the academy (the tier most people, including academic theologians, assume is "Real Theology"), and theology as it is done by all sorts and conditions of Christians, in their prayers, in their pews, at their pageants, during the liturgy, while reading the Bible or one of C. S. Lewis's books, yes, even while listening to their parish priest's sermon. There is a character in Molière's play *The City Gentleman* who exclaims, "Good heavens! For more than forty years I have been speaking prose without knowing it." In something like the same way, all Christians — including you, Christian reader — are theologians; it's just that you've been doing theology without knowing it.

So what is the purpose — what is the vocation — of a professional theologian like me? I think we need to remind ourselves of one important truth. Christian theology, the study of God in Christ, derives its subject-matter not directly from God but from the Church's witness to God. If there were no Church, no communities of Christian believers, there would be no Christian theology. Not that I question the importance and value of research, critical analysis, and systematic thought in theology. But it seems to me that a theologian cannot escape responsibility to the immediate source and ground of his or her study, that is, to the Church.

And what, pray, is the nature and character of this responsibility? Just this: that the theologian engage *and participate in* the witness of the Church. Or rather, that the theologian engage the Church's witness *through* participation in it, in order to enable and sustain the community and communion of the Church in owning its faith with genuine integrity, generation after generation. The critique that the theologian poses to the Church is not dissolvent but connective. That is, it invites, encourages, calls the community and communion of the Church to clarify its mind and connect its particular witness in this or that situation with the foundation of its faith, its confession of the love of God in Jesus Christ "poured into our hearts through the Holy Spirit" (Romans 5:5). The great Roman Catholic theologian Karl Rahner once defined the study of the history of dogma (or, as it is now fashionable to say, "historical theology") as "the art of reading texts in such a way that they become not just votes cast in favour of or against our current positions ..., but say something to us which we in our time have not considered at all, or not closely enough, about reality itself." By extension, the function of theology in the Church (and, I dare say, the academy) is the art of reading the Scriptures, the tradition, and the signs of the times in such a way as to speak that which the community and communion of the Church — and, yes, the academy — may not have considered at all, or not closely enough, about reality itself. Hence, the mandate of theologians is to participate in the witness of the Church, in such a way as to perform that witness itself, and thus be resources who assist the Church to a fuller, more genuine, more fruitful participation in its own mystery, the mystery of God in Christ.

Theology may also have a mandate to remind the community of the Church that we are called as much to what ancient teachers of the faith called *theôria*, the insight that is fruit of contemplation, as to busy practice. "Be still," the psalmist heard, "and know that I am God!" (Psalm 46:10). There are times and seasons, then, when it is not only appropriate but even necessary to ponder the mystery of God in Christ for its own sake, rather like Mount Everest, just because it's there. The passage — the passover — from Ash Wednesday through Palm Sunday to Easter Day and the Day of Pentecost, is the chief of such times and seasons. This is the one block of seasons above all when we are called to enter more deeply into the paschal mystery of Jesus Christ and share more fully in the communion of its meaning. In Lent, Holy Week, and Eastertide, a theologian may be of service to just this end; he or she may open the sluices of glory, so that we all may discover (or rediscover) the passion and resurrection of Jesus, and renew our own passing-over to God in him who is our Passover.

Such is my reason for offering this little collection to you. As I said at the beginning of this preface, my only ambition is that it may be a serviceable companion at your side. Dr. Reynolds does not presume to explain it all to you; he hopes merely to suggest some lines of thought that may prove fruitful as you take up the discipline recommended in the Ash Wednesday exhortation and "observe a holy Lent," Holy Week, and Eastertide by (among other things) "reading and meditating on the word of God."

It will become obvious to anyone who picks up this book that the meditations it contains seem to be a lot like sermons. Here an old adage may be paraphrased: If it looks like a sermon, walks like a sermon, and quacks like a sermon, it is a sermon. These meditations did indeed originate as sermons delivered during the seasons of Lent, Holy Week, and Easter over the course of the last fifteen years. In these years I have had the honour to serve four parish-communities in the Anglican Diocese of Toronto: as an honourary assistant and associate priest of the Church of St. Mary Magdalene, Toronto (1986–1992);

as interim priest-in-charge of the Church of St. Anne, Dufferin Street, Toronto (1991); as the incumbent of the Parish of Bridgenorth and Emily, on the eastern perimeter of the diocese (1993–1999); and as Theologian in Residence at the Church of the Redeemer, Toronto. The vast majority of the sermons included here were given in one or another of these four parishes.

Some may think it disingenuous of me to present a collection of *sermons* as a collection of *meditations*. It all depends on what you think a sermon should do, and what a meditation should be. My own approach to preaching (and, for that matter, teaching) is not to tell my listeners what they ought to think, but rather to invite them to consider one or another way of looking at a text, a doctrine, an image, a possibility; and my own style, both as writer and as speaker, tends to work by way of association more often than by way of linear argument. I like "strange loops." It may be merely an eccentricity of my mind and its imagination. But the result is, my sermons rarely try to "make a case"; they tend to be meditative, in the sense I spoke of earlier in this preface. A good sermon, in my view, is the fruit of meditation that, in turn, may become a seed of meditation in others' lives.

I have included two sermon-meditations of an occasional nature. The first, included in the section "Easter Season," is the sermon that I delivered at the funeral mass for Prudence Tracy in 1993. She was a very dear friend, and the godmother of our daughter Hannah. She died of cervical cancer on 21 April of that year; her requiem mass was celebrated at St. Mary Magdalene's three days later. I include it in this collection not only as the tribute of remembrance to a deeply cherished sister in Christ, but also with the pastoral awareness that many of us have suffered a loss, and the attendant grief, in the midst of the most joyous of all the Church's seasons. This sermon offers suggestions about mourning in Eastertide. The second occasional sermon-meditation is one that I preached at the ordination of a former student, Naomi Miller, to the priesthood on 2 April 2000. In that year, this was the Second Sunday of Lent; but I have included it in another section as a "coda" on Pentecost, because in it I sketched my understanding of priestly (and, by extension, ordained) ministry.

I have also included two meditational sermons delivered on Trinity Sunday. This seemed appropriate because the end of our passing-over will be to enter into the life of the God we worship and adore, as participants in the consort and polyphony of the three persons. As Augustine of Hippo confessed: "You have made us for yourself, and our hearts are restless until they rest in you."

Finally, I dedicate this collection to the people of the four parishes in which most of these sermons were preached. It is the lot of clergy and their families to know, over and over again, the condition of the stranger who seeks to belong to a new community. In each of these four parishes — St. Mary Magdalene's, St. Anne's, Bridgenorth and Emily, and the Church of the Redeemer — my wife, Mary, our daughter Hannah, and I have been able to murmur the blessing that the Son of Man will speak to those on his right hand: "We were strangers, and you welcomed us." More than that, in each successive community we found a home, where we had joy and gladness in the company of the people of God. If I truly served them as a priest, as a theologian, as a teacher and preacher, I hope that they will not mind if I offer these sermons to the wider community of the Church, in the hope that my words may also serve others.

SUGGESTIONS FOR USING THIS BOOK

This being a collection of meditations, it is meant to be dipped into, not read from cover to cover at one sitting — or, for that matter, even in one week. The most obvious way to dip into this book is to follow the rudimentary schedule suggested in the Table of Contents: there you will see, in parentheses following each title, the Sunday or weekday to which each meditation properly belongs. Start with the first, "Ash Wednesday," then simply read each meditation in the sequence of the seasons, one per week or (as in Holy Week) one per day.

There are a number of meditations that belong to the same Sunday, though in different years of the Revised Common Lectionary's three-year cycle (A, B, C). You might read each of these entries in its proper year, one a year; or you might read the entry for the proper year in the cycle on the eve of the Sunday (Saturday afternoon or evening), and read the other two during the course of the following week. For example, in Year B of the RCL, you might read "The Wedding Covenant" on the Third Sunday of Lent; then read "The Conversion of Dust" on (say) Tuesday, and "Naming God" on Thursday or Friday.

There are other meditations that deal with the same texts; these I have listed by numerals rather than by years. The procedure I just suggested might also be used in these cases — for example, read "Sight (*Fourth Sunday of Lent*, Year A, 1)" on the day itself (or its eve), and "God's Spittle (*Fourth Sunday of Lent*, 2)" and "The Ways of God (*Fourth Sunday of Lent*, Year A, 3)" on different days during the course of the following week.

Lent

ASH WEDNESDAY

Since the children share flesh and blood, [Jesus] himself like-
wise shared the same things, so that through death he might
destroy the one who has the power of death, that is, the devil,
and free those who all their lives were held in slavery by the
fear of death.

(HEBREWS 2:14–15)

Today the Church puts on ashes. Ashes are a sign of grief, grief that we ourselves have grieved the Holy One, and grieved other humans, by our sinning. So, by putting on ashes today, we bear a sacrament of our sorrow for not loving God with our whole heart, and for not loving our neighbours as ourselves.

But ashes mark not only our sorrow. They also speak "of the frailty and uncertainty of human life." "Our days are like the grass," says the psalmist; "we flourish like a flower of the field. When the wind goes over it, it is gone, and its place shall know it no more" (Psalm 103:15–16). And so, when a priest imposes the ashes on our foreheads, the Church appoints these words to be said and heard: "Remember that you are dust, and to dust shall you return." On Ash Wednesday, ashes are meant to be a sign of our mortality.

And therein lies the root of our sins — the desire to escape that mortality, a desire to shimmy out of the inevitability of our death. These escapes are always vain because their motive is fear. We want to get away from the gulag of death, but have no notion of where we should escape *to*. Indeed, as soon as we seem to be out of the prison, we find that our sanctuary is just another tunnel of mortality; we have burrowed only more deeply into our slavery.

So today we stop pretending: we admit that we are mortal, that we were formed from dust and to that same dust we shall return. By accepting the sign of ashes on this Wednesday, the fortieth day before Easter, we take responsibility for our frailty, for the pains of our humanity. Not that we thereby announce our intention to do something about it, to get rid of the frailty and stop feeling the pains. No, what we signify by this sign of ashes is our willingness to look our frailty and our pains squarely in the face — and to carry on, with courage and love and faithfulness, not in spite of the frailty but in light of the frailty. With this new or renewed knowledge of our condition — with this new or renewed *honesty* about our condition — we are able to do what we must without kidding ourselves.

Having admitted our frailty and our mortality, then, we await our liberation. For freedom comes not through escape, but only through the liberation of the country in which the prison stands. And that is what Christ did in his paschal mystery, in the mystery of his passover from suffering through death to the resurrection. The Letter to the Hebrews says: "Since the children share flesh and blood," the Lord Jesus "likewise partook of the same nature, that through death he might destroy him who has the power of death, and deliver all those who through fear of death were subject to lifelong bondage. The Lord did not escape our mortality. On the contrary, he accepted death in all its horror. And yet, God liberated him — and through him, has liberated us too.

Through Christ Jesus, God has liberated the whole countryside of the human condition. What we could never finally escape, he himself has overthrown. So, today, we accept the reality of our bondage to death, but no longer in fear. For we know that the land has already been liberated, and that our gulag is now, through the mercy of the Paschal Lamb, become a transit camp on the way to the glorious liberty of the children of God.

And that is why, on this Wednesday, we receive not only the sign of ashes, but also another sign — the double sign of bread and cup. For this sign, the conjoint sign of bread and cup, means Jesus Christ, the true and living Bread who came down from heaven. This is food for people in transit, for people who are passing over from the gulag of fear to the liberty of God in Christ. By tasting these signs of bread and cup, we also taste him, who is our Passover, the firstborn of the new creation. And just as he shared all the frailty of our humanity, so, by the mercy of God, we may come to share the glory of his divinity — and there is no frailty in God, who is "always the same, and whose years shall never end" (Psalm 102:27). So with the sign of ashes, which speaks of the frailty and uncertainty of human life, and marks the penitence of the Christian community as a whole, we also receive the sign of Christ, which marks the forgiveness of all our sins and speaks of the glory that shall be ours in him.

So then, let us use this Lent to prepare for our passage, our passover, not by devising clever ruses for escape, but by learning the ways of God's liberty and the practice of that freedom for which Christ has set us free.

THE REFINING
PROCESS

*Jesus was led up by the Spirit into the wilderness to be tempted
by the devil.*

(MATTHEW 4:1)

At the very beginning of his career, "Jesus was led up by the Spirit into the wilderness to be tempted by the devil." So says St. Matthew; and he gives us an imaginative account of the Lord's experience of temptation at the hand of Satan. The story is loaded with unlikely details. But even before we get to these details, we may be puzzled by the starting point of the story — that the only Son of God was in fact *tempted*. That sounds like a contradiction in terms; for how could Jesus, who was supposed to be the very pitch of perfection, be so imperfect as to feel temptations?

We have all been brought up to think that there is something wrong with us when we feel tempted to stray from the straight and narrow — indeed, that there's something wrong with us *because* we feel temptation. We do not even have to commit a sin; we have fallen just in thinking the thought, just in feeling the feeling, just in having to fight the instinct or the enticement. Never mind the actual sin: merely to be tempted to do it is itself a mark of failure, because it exposes our weaknesses and betrays the wobbliness of our wills.

But this very attitude, so common among Christians, was not shared by St. Matthew the evangelist. On the contrary, Matthew seems to regard temptation as something that Jesus *had* to experience — and Jesus had to be tempted not *in spite of* his being God's only Son, but *because* he was God's only Son. The very fact that Jesus was tempted was a sign that our common enemy, Satan, had recognized his enemy; and their encounter was not a mark of Jesus' weakness, but a trial of his strength, a test of his commitment to the will and purpose of the Father who sent him.

Seen in that light, the temptations of Jesus in the wilderness were not evidence of weakness in an otherwise perfect nature. They were like the refining of silver or gold in a crucible: the ore is put into a fiery furnace, so that all the dross may be burned away until nothing is left but the pure metal. Just so, Jesus was set in the heat of the wilderness and put to the test, so that he might prove his mettle as the true Son of God; and afterwards nothing was left in him but pure obedience to the saving purpose of his Father in heaven.

That is how we should regard our own times of temptation — not as enticements that betray our weakness, but as a refining process by which the ore of our baptism is purified in us, until nothing is left but the gold of loving obedience to God. No one says that this process is easy to bear or gentle upon our faith; but still, there is indeed something infinitely precious in us, something infinitely precious to the same infinite God who placed it there — and this God will never destroy, nor allow to be destroyed, what God's own hand has created in us.

Through our temptations, then, we may reveal our truth and worth as children of God, as brothers and sisters of the only Son of God — even as Jesus demonstrated that he was the very Son of God during those forty days in the wilderness, tempted by the devil. So, do not heed the heat of the trial, but rejoice in the God who is seeking to manifest his Son in us more and more, until we are stamped with the eternal image of Christ and our very lives and personalities are minted as the pure gold coin of God's realm.

TESTING

(MARK 1:9–15)

JESUS "was baptized by John in the Jordan," and then "the Spirit immediately drove him out into the wilderness. He was in the wilderness forty days, tempted by Satan." So the gospel of Mark tells us. One thing about the story may stand out as curious — the insistence that Jesus was in the wilderness forty days. This insistence on the forty days stands out because that is just the length of the Lenten fast; and the Church imposes on itself this forty-day preparation for Easter in imitation of its Lord's forty days in the wilderness. And perhaps our curiosity is piqued by this specification of days. Why *forty* days? Why not seven days or fourteen, why not thirty days or sixty? The answer is embedded in the witness of Scripture itself; and the answer has to do with the pattern of salvation that God has designed for us.

Forty was one of those numbers that ancient peoples considered to be fraught with mystical meaning. It was a number to conjure with — quite literally, a number that worked magic. The ancient Hebrews adopted this belief about the number forty, but then transformed its significance. In their reckoning, forty did not contain magic. Instead, it represented the days of God's wrath and the co-ordinates of Israel's repentance. For after the people Israel came out of Egypt, they were in the wilderness forty years; and those forty years were punishment for their grumbling, their murmuring, their disobedience against the Lord their God. The forty-day temptation of Jesus can be seen in the light of Israel's forty years of waywardness in Sinai. By his obedience to God during those days, Jesus reversed the meaning of that earlier experience; indeed, where Israel had failed, Jesus fulfilled the commandments; and so, by his forty days in the wilderness, Jesus proved himself to be the true Israel, the authentic child of God.

That is one interpretation. But the Church asks us to look elsewhere for the meaning of the forty days, to another and much earlier sign of forty. It asks us to ponder the story of Noah and the great flood — the forty days when eight human beings and two of every other kind of creature experienced not wrath but salvation. True, all the rest of creation was supposed to have been destroyed; but that is not the point of the story. The point of the story is that Noah and all the rest in the ark were saved. Their forty days upon the flood were not a revelation of wrath but a sign of redemption. And so it is with the forty days that Jesus was tempted in the wilderness: his testing was not a mark of punishment, but a proof of salvation. As Noah's ark stood the test of forty days in a wilderness of water, so Jesus went forth from his baptism and anointing and stood the test of forty days in the wilderness of Judea. Jesus himself is the new ark; an ark made of humanity, not wood, and made of a humanity so seasoned that he is able to bear all creation in the embrace of his crucified arms.

In this we may see the reason for our own forty days, and the meaning of Lent. It is not a season of punishment, when we must hurt our humanity lest God hurt it for us. No, Lent is a time of redemption, when we season our humanity that God may build us into Christ. And being built into Christ, we may have his strength to shape creation, not just our own private selves, but the fearful, imperilled, and anxious crowd of creation, in its cry for mercy and in its plea for justice. So let us begin these forty days as Noah, that we may end them with Christ.

LEAVING HOME, GOING HOME

Now the Lord said to Abram, "Go from your country and your kindred and your father's house to the land that I will show you. I will make of you a great nation, and I will bless you, and make your name great, so that you will be a blessing."

(GENESIS 12:1–2)

The wind blows where it chooses, and you hear the sound of it, but you do not know where it comes from or where it goes. So it is with everyone who is born of the Spirit.

(JOHN 3:8)

WHEN I WAS a child, my family moved to a new house in a new town quite frequently. The number and the tempo of the moves slowed down as the years passed; indeed, when I was teenager, we moved to a house where my parents stayed a full seventeen years before pulling up stakes again. But still, when I was a youngster, we moved to a new house in a new town on an average of every three years. Perhaps that is why I hate the very idea of moving to a new place. It is not the aggravation of packing, or the seemingly endless job of unpacking, so much as the instability that a move always involves. When I get someplace, I want to stay there; I entrench myself in that place with friendships and all the things I like to have around me, and I begin generating memories.

So it comes as unwelcome news to hear Jesus say, "The wind blows where it chooses, and you hear the sound of it, but you do not know where it comes from or where it goes. So it is with everyone who is born of the Spirit." The Church has chosen to interpret this saying through some verses from the book of Genesis and a passage from the Letter of Paul to the Romans, which together remind us of the story of Abraham. For Abraham obeyed God's command and left his own country, his own kindred, and his father's house, to become like the wind — to follow God wherever God might send him. And Abraham's faith, Abraham's trust in God's promise, "was reckoned to him as righteousness" (Genesis 15:6). Abraham did not dig himself in; he acted on the gust of God's Spirit, even though he did not know where that gust of the Spirit would take him.

There are a number of ways of reading Abraham's decision. One reading would see Abraham's move as a declaration of independence, as a sign that believers should go with the flow and be footloose, ready to act on the immediate urges of personal integrity and self-expression. But another reading — a truer reading — would understand Abraham's upping stakes as an act of obedience. For Abraham did not leave his own country and his father's house, he did not renounce the security of his own tribe and his heritage, just because he thought it might be a good idea. He was not expressing his own freedom; he was obeying God's will and relying on the promise of the God "who gives life to the dead and calls into existence the things that do not exist" (Romans 4:17).

The story of Abraham is a story of obedience, such obedience that he was willing to pull up his roots and go wherever

God led. And so it is with the life of all who have received the Holy Spirit, who for the sake of following God become like "the wind [which] blows where it chooses, and you hear the sound of it, but you do not know where it comes from or where it goes."

But this willingness to move when and as God wills is not a matter of having no roots at all. It is a matter of letting our lives be rooted in God and God alone. To those who define themselves by places and the memories associated with them, such obedience will always appear to be the very opposite of obedience; it will make us appear footloose and fancy-free, even whimsical and fickle. That is because our true homeland, the homeland to which God calls us and guides us, is not a place in this world; it is not a spot where we may dig in and entrench ourselves. It is heaven — and heaven is just another way of speaking about the glory of God, that glory that has no boundaries to limit its power, no walls to partition its beauty, no need of floors to steady its majesty, and no ceiling to the abundance of its life.

This is the land, this is the life, to which we are being led by the Spirit of God who gave new birth in baptism; and this is the homeland, the true native country, the glory for which we must practise the obedience of Abraham — the sort of obedience that is ready to pull up roots in this world at the word of God's call and in response to Christ's promise that we shall find an eternal dwelling not only in the neighbourhood of God but even within the glory of God's own life.

Abraham's Laughter

The word of the Lord came to Abram in a vision, "Do not be afraid, Abram, I am your shield; your reward shall be very great." But Abram said, "O Lord God, what will you give me, for I continue childless, and the heir of my house is Eliezer of Damascus?... You have given me no offspring, and so a slave born in my house is to be my heir." But the word of the Lord came to him, "This man shall not be your heir; no one but your very own issue shall be your heir." He brought him outside and said, "Look toward heaven and count the stars, if you are able to count them." Then he said to him, "So shall your descendants be." And he believed the Lord; and the Lord reckoned it to him as righteousness.

(Genesis 15:1–6)

At the beginning of the eucharist, we ask the Lord, we ask Christ, to have mercy upon us. The story of Abraham and Sarah suggests why we cry for this mercy. For is the story of an elderly couple who have no child of their own, and whose future had become a matter of remembrance, not of action? Yet God came to Abram, changed his name to Abraham, which means "Father of a multitude," and gave him and his wife the power of a future, the power to have a child. And, as St. Paul said, even though Abraham's body was as good as dead, yet he was "fully convinced that God was able to do what he promised" (Romans 4:21) — he trusted in God to have mercy on his weakness, on the sorrow of his aging body. For such is the mercy of this God, that he even "gives life to the dead and calls into existence things that do not exist" (Romans 4:17).

It is important to remember that Abraham was an upright man, just in his dealings with God and with other humans. Thus sin is not the issue in God's mercy toward him. The issue is the ordinary weaknesses of being a human, being a creature that ages and changes, feels hunger and thirst, and is frail in body and spirit. To be sure, we should recall and confess our sins, and ask mercy from the divine Judge. But we should also remember that sin is, first and foremost, the way we deal with our creatureliness — or rather, the way we refuse to deal with it, our way of denying that we are indeed frail beings, creatures who did not make themselves, but were made by God. So, before we can deal with our sins, we must face our humanity, own up to it, yes, and place it before the God who gave it to us.

And that is just what Abraham did. Indeed, it was part of his righteousness that, even as he lay on his face before the presence of God Almighty, he laughed. He laughed at the idea that a child could be born to a man who was a hundred years old, at the idea that a woman who was ninety years old could bear a child. But Abraham's laughter was not the cackle of doubt; it was the chuckle of someone who has just heard something too good to be true. He did not want to push his luck — or put God to the test. So he laughed, as if to wake himself up from a dream.

But it was all true: God really was promising to give Abraham and Sarah a child of their own; and the birth of this child would be the sign that God had made a covenant with Abraham. Now, covenant is just a fancy word for a bargain, a deal; and so God struck a bargain, made a deal with Abraham and Sarah, that they would be the ancestors of a multitude of nations, and that their descendants would inhabit and own the land where Abraham and Sarah themselves were only nomads and transients. But there is something funny about this covenant. Normally a bargain requires give and take on both sides: "You do this for me, and I will do that for you." But there is no tit-for-tat in the bargain that God makes with Abraham and Sarah. It is all on God's side; Abraham and Sarah do not have to do anything in return, except continue to do what they had been doing all along — walk in the ways of God, and be faithful to this God. No wonder Abraham laughed; he was being offered the deal of a lifetime; a deal wherein God showered all his almighty mercy upon Abraham and Sarah, and all they had to do was ... just take it.

Now, we are the children of Abraham and Sarah; and God's covenant with them continues with us. When we look at ourselves, at our numbers, our options, even our expectations of ourselves, we might well laugh, the way Abraham did: "Who — *us*? God has made a covenant with *us*?" Yes, God has made a covenant with us, that together as a church we should inherit the meaning of Abraham's name and be "ancestor of a multitude" — yes, of a multitude right here in this place. Such is the bargain that the Almighty strikes with us today; and all we have to do is believe in the mercy that strikes the bargain.

The God who made us knows that we are only human, and knows that in him alone we live and move and have our being; and he asks us to know the same truth, even — or especially — when we feel the weakness of what we are. Thus, as a modern writer, Gail Ramshaw, has said: "The word 'mercy' means God's compassion, the compassion humanity needs if it is to survive in the face of evil and before the face of God. We do not stand up well before either death or divinity. And so we cry for mercy. We ask God to be more gracious than magnificent, more forgiving than righteous. We plead for release from the pains of our humanity." And God, who hears the plea of the creature, will indeed have mercy. For this same God made the world out of nothing, and formed our humanity when as yet there was no such thing; this is the same God who gave Abraham and Sarah a child even though their bodies were "already as good as dead," and the very same God who gave life to his crucified Son and brought him forth again from the utter frailty of death, from entombment in the earth. God's covenant of mercy and new life continues, and it continues with us, if we have but faith to sign our lives on the dotted line.

MISPLACED SELVES

Those who want to save their life will lose it, and those who lose their life for my sake, and for the sake of the gospel, will save it. For what will it profit them to gain the whole world and forfeit their life?

(MARK 8:35–36)

Just the other night, while Mary was at the weekly rehearsal of the choir that she belongs to, I sat down in front of the television with two baskets of laundry and began to sort and fold. There is something very satisfying about folding laundry: it can give you a sense of what it means to be in the image and likeness of God. For out of this chaos of clothing you create order, and behold, it is very good. Except, that particular night, I came up with no less than eight socks — eight of *my* socks — that had no partners. I knew that there was a small pile of other stray socks upstairs on my dresser, so I went to get them and brought them back down. That took five minutes. It took another ten minutes to sort through the two piles. I matched exactly three pairs — and now found myself with eleven stray socks on my hands. Fifteen more minutes were spent looking for a flashlight so that I could inspect the inner recesses of the washer and dryer; and the inspection took another seven. By this point I had missed the greater part of the show I had been watching, and hadn't a clue about the way the plot had developed, or why. So I picked up my notes for the next day's lecture. But could I find the pencil I'd been using? *Nooo* — I had misplaced that too. Never mind, I told myself, I'll just get another from that box of pencils ... somewhere. When I found the box and pulled out a pencil, I needed a sharpener. Only, it was not where I usually keep it. It looked as if my whole life was being deposited, one item at a time, in the cosmic lost-and-found department. Just then, Mary returned from her rehearsal and rescued me from my maelstrom of misplacements. I had spent close to ninety minutes hunting for things I wanted but could not find.

That night's comedy was unusual for the sheer number of things I could not find; but it strikes me that the experience itself was not really all so very unusual — on the contrary, it was more typical of the human lot than we care to admit. For we spend up to half our lives looking for things we have misplaced in the ordinary course of the other half. We know right where that book, or pair of scissors, or file, or jewel, or potato-peeler *should* be — it should be right where you're *sure* you put it the last time you used it — but it's not there now. And because you cannot finish doing your task without it, you spend the next little while rummaging through all your other belongings to find it. Of course, even if you do find it — even if you find it fairly quickly — it is frequently no longer of any use to you, because the time spent searching for it has broken your concentration, evaporated your train of thought, or even diverted your attention to some other matter.

These maddening little episodes are accidents of life, rather like stumbling over an unnoticed frost-heave in the sidewalk or missing the bottom step of a stairway. We mutter a curse, and carry on; our sense of perspective tells us that these missteps and misplacements do not really matter in the long run, for accidents by definition have no purpose and, without a purpose, can have no meaning.

But I wonder … I wonder if we misplace items by accident. Divine providence is a mystery; and it is often hard to discern God's hand in what happens to us and in the world around us. But what if most of the obscurity that we ascribe to God's purpose arises not from God but from ourselves? We humans are so solemn about our lives, that we assume God — and the mystery of God's care and control of the universe — must be eternally solemn as well. It may be a mistake to think so. For the omnipotence of the Almighty may be elfin. God has a sense of humour; and we are so shocked by the idea — it is so very impolite even to think such a thought — that we are doomed never to get the joke. God, they say, is in the details. So it is a fancy of mine — take it for what it's worth — it is a fancy I have, that the Most High likes to upset our solemnity by misplacing the odd items of everyday life — a box of paper-clips here, a floppy disk there, a flashlight or a potato-peeler, our car keys or a rake, one of a pair of cuff-links, or single socks. By inconveniencing us in these mundane matters, the three-person'd God hopes to convenience us for glory. For the point of the divine joke is not to show us how absent-minded we are, but to suggest that we are not absent-minded enough. The problem is not that we misplace things; the problem is, we fail to misplace the one thing we should.

In the gospel Jesus says: "Those who want to save their life will lose it, and those who lose their life for my sake, and for the sake of the gospel, will save it. For what will it profit them to gain the whole world and forfeit their life?" We save things — rooms full of books, basements and garages and closets full of gadgets, bank accounts and investments, newspapers and magazines, CDs and videos and DVDs, houses and cars and gardens — we hoard these things in order to make our presence in the world have (or at least, appear to have) more substance. Of course, the more we hoard, the more likely we are to misplace and lose things. Perhaps that is why we get so fretful, and some of us become so obsessive, about finding the one item we have misplaced. By the sudden unavailability of that one item, we imagine that a portion of our presence in the world has slipped away; and we are afraid not for the missing item but for our solemn selves. By the hard, the paradoxical saying about losing and saving, Jesus calls us to let go of the fear by letting go of the delusion that makes the fear possible — the delusion that our presence in the world is only as substantial as the things we hoard around us. If that is our attitude, Jesus is saying, we shall find everything lost in the end; our presence will become absolutely insubstantial, for we shall be as wraiths that God does not see so much as see through, almost as if we were not there.

What alternative does Jesus propose? "Those who lose their life for my sake, and for the sake of the gospel, will save it." The Lord is not telling us to renounce all our belongings; he is telling us to lose our lives — as it were, to stop misplacing things by accident and learn to misplace our selves deliberately. Something misplaced is something in a place other than where we thought it should be. Our lives take place in the world, and we think that by gathering things around us we will find them there. But we deceive ourselves. It is only by placing our selves in another — first of all, in Jesus and in the good news of his life, and then, for his sake, at the disposal of one another — that we shall find our true selves and become genuinely substantial in presence.

We are said to be in the image and likeness of God. We never live up to that image so fully, nor ever enact that likeness so graciously, as when we learn to imitate the divine sense of humour. God, I say, "misplaces" the items we want in order to sting us into a just perspective. So may we "misplace" our selves in Jesus, that we find our lives sinewy with the substance of his glory.

OUR LOWLY BODY

But our citizenship is in heaven, and it is from there that we are expecting a Saviour, the Lord Jesus Christ. He will transform the body of our humiliation that it may be conformed to the body of his glory, by the power that also enables him to make all things subject to himself.

(PHILIPPIANS 3:20–21)

L ENT IS the season when the Church encourages us to adopt certain habits, to enrich our own lives and the life of this Christian community, to deepen and strengthen the reflexes of Christ in ourselves and in our world, for the sake of celebrating Easter more richly when it comes. So it is odd that we often should regard Lent, not as a time of enrichment, but almost exclusively as a season of bodily self-denial — as if our bodies victimized our souls, rather than the other way around, and as if depressing ourselves physically were alone sufficient for preparing ourselves spiritually.

St. Paul appears to lend support to this view. For he laments the condition of those who "live as enemies of the cross of Christ" (Philippians 3:18) — those who make a god out of their own appetites, who have "their minds ... set on earthly things" (Philippians 3:19). Then Paul goes on to say that we Christians are different, because "our citizenship," our native city, the society to which we really belong, is "in heaven" — and it is from heaven that "we are expecting a Saviour, the Lord Jesus Christ," who "will transform the body of our humiliation that it may be conformed to the body of his glory." So there it is, and right from the Apostle's mouth: our body manifests our humiliation, that is, the lowliness of our condition, the humbled, depressed, even shrunken state of our humanity. And we might draw the conclusion, that since our body partakes of, even as it manifests, "our humiliation," it deserves to be depressed and deprived even further. But before we settle on this conclusion, let us consider whether it is what the Apostle really intended.

First of all, it needs to be said that when Paul associated the body with "our humiliation," he did not mean us to feel ashamed of being physical beings, as if it were not only just too vulgar but also downright shameful for us to have such a thing as a body. That is not what Paul meant. When he spoke of "the body of our humiliation," he was referring to what was (for him) just a fact of human life, whose moral value could be either good or bad, depending on circumstances. For Paul, the human body is humble, even humiliated, because humanity as a whole has humble origins.

Adam is the key. In the story of creation, Adam was formed from the earth — indeed, his very name comes from the Hebrew word *adamah*, meaning "earth," as in the ground underneath our feet. Adam was an earthy being, as earthy as the soil you roto-till and dig in springtime. So, when Paul spoke of "the body of our humiliation," he meant, in part, that we live our life close to the earth from which it was formed, a life that, from high up, looks as if it were creeping and crawling along the ground; a life that, even at eye-level, appears hunched over and bent toward the earth. When you go to a mall, or walk the streets, notice how many people move with their heads down and their eyes on the sidewalk or floor. Why do people have such a posture? Some may do so out of the natural reflex of self-defence, in order to bulldoze their way through the human horde that is even then bulldozing its way toward them. But too many people walk with their heads down and eyes on the ground even when there is no crowd, to make this the only or even the best explanation. Perhaps such a posture is a deeper part of our nature than even self-defence, because our body really is lowly, in the sense of being attracted to the earth from which our life was fashioned.

The Apostle means that our body is lowly in a further way, in a sense that extends our earthiness. Load your hands with bags full of groceries, and your shoulders will begin to slouch, your back will hunch, and your head will loll toward the ground as your neck acts like a lever against the weight of your packages. You have become a beast of burden, truly a "lowly" creature. And that is also what Paul means: not only is our body "lowly" because our nature is slung low to the ground, to the earth that old Adam comes from. Our body also manifests the humiliating pains of our humanity, burdened as it is by colds and the 'flu, by everyday exhaustion and extraordinary ills, by bruises inflicted on flesh and spirit. Is it mere coincidence that when we are doing poorly, we say we are "feeling low"? Our life does indeed "cleave to the dust," because it sags and is made low under the burdens that it is forced to bear; and the sagging is a humiliation. Such a condition is not sin, it is not something to be ashamed of; it is just the way we are.

Finally, our body is lowly by comparison with another body — by comparison with "the body of Christ's glory." Paul means that "the body of our humiliation" shall be set on high — it shall be made to stand erect at its full height and dignity beside the risen Lord, hand in hand with him before the face of the living God. As Paul says elsewhere, our nature will undergo a tremendous change. "The first man [Adam] was from the earth, a man of dust; the second man [Christ] is from heaven.... And just as we have borne the image of the man of dust, we will also bear the image of the man of heaven" (1 Corinthians 15:47, 49). Our body, which by nature cleaves to the dust, shall be raised up in the likeness of the risen Christ, so that it may cleave to the light of the glory of God.

It shall be a marvellous conversion; and this conversion is our hope, our faith, our desire; it is the life's breath of the Church and the whole point of being a Christian. And, yes, it is the whole point of the eucharist. At the words and gestures of our beseeching, God receives our gifts of bread and wine and converts their lowly body, changes their earthy nature, to become the mystery of the glorious body and blood of Christ; and we in turn receive this heavenly gift, so that our own lowly body may be converted, our earthly nature may be changed more and more, into the likeness of Christ's glory. Now that glory is veiled in this sacramental mystery, so that hereafter it may be manifested in our bodies.

All this is from God, who created us and loves us and, yes, calls us to be different from those whose minds are set on earthly things, on the *adamah*, the ground from which Adam was formed. In this Lenten season let us lift our drooping heads and straighten our burdened shoulders, let us look up from the earth, and taste by faith what our eyes shall drink in with undimmed vision, when we shall be able to sing in truth and not just in sacrament, "Blessed is he who comes in the Name of the Lord!" — when Christ shall have transformed the body of our humiliation and the lowliness of our condition, and conformed that body to the body of his glory, even as he raises our humanity to share in and enjoy the citizenship with which baptism endued us, as naturalized citizens of the city of God, exercising to the full the franchise of heaven.

GOD AND GRASSHOPPERS

Have you not known? Have you not heard?
Has it not been told you from the beginning?
Have you not understood from the foundations of the earth?

It is he who sits above the circle of the earth,
and its inhabitants are like grasshoppers....

But those who wait for the Lord shall renew their strength,
they shall mount up with wings like eagles,

they shall run and not be weary,
they shall walk and not faint.

(ISAIAH 40:21–22, 31)

I belong to the smallest minority group in Canada: I am a Canadian who likes winter. Or at least I used to. Several weeks ago, I became a fully assimilated Canadian and joined the whining and complaining majority. It was during that snap of slicing winds and flesh-congealing cold; like almost everybody else, I could not escape the chill, no matter how many layers of clothing I wore, no matter where I was. It happened to be on Thursday morning of that week, while standing in a packed subway train going to work, when I noticed that not even the company of so many people afforded any relief from the cold. It was then that I started to have reveries of summer — not of last summer or the summer before, but of summers now long ago and far away. I think of a boy sitting in the breezeway of an old farmhouse that sat on the crest of a hill, surrounded by fields and re-encroaching woodland; and from the vantage of that breezeway, that boy used to look across the street, over the rim of a stone wall, into the sun-seared field beyond. The field looked perfectly still in the glare of the afternoon's humidity; but the boy knew that it couldn't be as still as it looked. For from that very field came the monotony — something between a twitter and a clack — of several hundred grasshoppers rubbing their legs. The sound of that sight — the clacking twitter of all those invisible grasshoppers rising from that field in the stillness of an August heat-wave — has defined summer time for the adult who came of that boy; and that is what my memory heard and saw — and lusted after — on that subway train in cruellest January.

But then, such memories of August may be more than just fantasies in January, and the summer-lust that Canadians experience every winter may be a reflection of far greater things than our chilled imaginations think. Consider an image that the prophet Isaiah gives us:

"It is [God] who sits above the circle of the earth, and its inhabitants are like grasshoppers...."

(ISAIAH 40:22)

The prophet is asking us to ponder the utter sovereignty of the Almighty over all creation — and the utter insignificance of creatures by comparison. Just as that boy once sat in the shade of a breezeway on the crest of a hill, so God rocks in his throne under the bowers of glory, the book of life open on his lap, looking over the wall of paradise, into the created universe beyond; and it is an expanse so vast that it seems as still as a sun-blistered field on a humid summer's afternoon. And yet it is not still, for from that field of creation God hears the clacking twitter of its human inhabitants, the way humans hear grasshoppers rub their legs.

This image is not designed to compliment us or heighten our sense of dignity and self-worth. Grasshoppers are okay in their way, and certainly have a right to exist; but they are, after all, only bugs. The prophet is asking us to set our minds in the breezeway of heaven, and see and hear ourselves from God's perspective — as creatures that are okay in their way, and that certainly have a right to exist, but are, after all, only humans, small beings who are so deeply involved in the strands of the universe that we should be unnoticeable, but for the drone we give off in the heat of our little day.

And just what is our drone, the clacking twitter we make as we rub body and soul together the way grasshoppers rub their legs? It is a whining complaint, such as the prophet heard:

Why do you say, O Jacob,
  and speak, O Israel,
"My way is hidden from the Lord,
  and my right is disregarded by my God"?
(ISAIAH 40:27)

The grasshopper does not clack in the fields in order to complain about our indifference to its presence; as far as we know, the grasshopper's noise is a sound of rejoicing. But we rustle our souls because we think God does not care about us, disregards us, ignores us; and ironically the monotonous clacking of our little beings is usually a signal we send to one another to console our own selves, not a prayer we send to God to gain compassion for our negligibility.

If that is the irony of our complaint, it is compounded by another irony — by an irony that so far transcends irony as to become positively funny. For the prophet bears witness that God *does* care about us grasshoppers; it is the very measure of the magnificence of God's sovereignty, that the Almighty attends to the drone of the creature.

> Have you not known? Have you not heard?
> The Lord is the everlasting God,
> the Creator of the ends of the earth....
>
> He gives power to the faint,
> and strengthens the powerless....
>
> [and] those who wait for the Lord shall renew their
> strength,
> they shall mount up with wings like eagles.
>
> (ISAIAH 40:28, 29, 31)

All the awesome power of the divine Creator is at the disposal of the enfeebled, and the infinite strength of the Everlasting is flexed in those who have no power at all. Grasshoppers shall become eagles, and mortal humans shall mount up to "become participants of the divine nature" (2 Peter 1:4).

It is a rule of the lectionary that we use, in appointing the readings for each Sunday, that the reading from the Old Testament and the reading from the gospel should be related to one another in theme. And the theme we heard in the prophet Isaiah — the Almighty's care for us grasshoppers — is borne out in today's reading from Mark's gospel (Mark 1:29–39). There we heard about the cluster of healings and exorcisms that Jesus performed at Capernaum — how he healed Simon's mother-in-law of her fever, then "cured many who were sick with various diseases, and cast out many demons" (Mark 1:30–34A). We might see these miracles as the fulfilment of the prophet's word about God "giving power to the faint, and strengthening the powerless"; and within the terms of Mark's gospel, we would not be far off base. But it is in the sequel to these miracles that Jesus acts most like the One "who sits above the circle of the earth," and heeds the drone of its inhabitant grasshoppers. For the morning after the healings and exorcisms, "while it was still very dark, Jesus got up and went out to a deserted place," to the rim of the world, above the circle of creation, "and there he prayed." But not for long; if there is no rest for the wicked, there is even less rest for the Son of God. For his disciples "hunted for him," and "when they found him, they said to him, 'Everyone is searching for you' " (Mark 1:35–37). The twittering clack of our grasshopper selves continues, and it is still directed at one another rather than at the one everyone seeks; only "Simon and his companions" have the sense — or is it the grace? — actually to go looking for him. "Jesus answered, 'Let us go on to the neighbouring towns, so that I may proclaim the message there also; for that is what I came out to do' " (Mark 1:38). He "came to seek out and to save the lost" (Luke 19:10), those who "wandered in desert wastes," and could find "no way to a city where they might dwell," so that "their spirits languished within them" (Psalm 107:4, 5); he came to hear their cry — and not only by working miracles for them, but also by "proclaiming the message" that would unpack the meaning of the miracles. The clacking, self-referential word of complaint rising monotonously from the field of the world, whose "inhabitants are like grasshoppers," is met by the Word made flesh, who no longer "sits above the circle of the earth," but wades into the field to address a divine, human-oriented message of promise to those very same inhabitants.

And therein is our dignity; not in the noise we send out in the heat of our little day, but in the descent of one who sits above the circle of the earth, to take our complaining seriously, even more seriously than we take it ourselves, and not only to act but also to act with a word, a message of salvation. We might twitter against the prophet's call to ponder our lives from God's perspective and take umbrage at being compared with grasshoppers; but then we will miss the awesome truth, that the sovereign of the universe really does care for us, so much so that the infinite gap between the breezeway of heaven and the field of this world has vanished. For God the Word has crossed the gap, climbed over the fence, and walked in our field, to give us a word in response to our twittering clack, the word that shall make us grasshoppers mount up as eagles.

THE CONVERSION OF DUST

Jesus answered her, "If you knew the gift of God, and who it is that is saying to you, 'Give me a drink,' you would have asked him, and he would have given you living water." The woman said to him, "Sir, you have no bucket, and the well is deep. Where do you get that living water? Are you greater than our ancestor Jacob, who gave us the well, and with his sons and his flocks drank from it?" Jesus said to her, "Everyone who drinks of this water will be thirsty again, but those who drink of the water that I will give them will never be thirsty. The water that I will give will become in them a spring of water gushing up to eternal life." The woman said to him. "Sir, give me this water, so that I may never be thirsty or have to keep coming here to draw water."

(JOHN 4:10–15)

When God had a mind to make human beings, says the book of Genesis, the Almighty formed us out of "dust from the ground." Dust from the ground … not a solid lump of clay, not even a mass of wet sand by the seashore, but only flecks of dried-out earth, mere particles from the scalp of creation. That is our nature; and that is what we try to understand about ourselves on Ash Wednesday, when many of us receive the sign of ashes with the stark words, "Remember that you are dust, and to dust shall you return."

The earth turns to dust wherever there is a persistent lack of moisture — wherever the earth has been stripped of its trees and grass and it has no protection against the sun and the wind, nothing to draw up the water from below or to call for the rain from above. So dust is always thirsty, it always needs a drink. And even when it does get a drink, it cannot hold the moisture within itself; it soon dries out once more, and becomes thirsty all over again. And so it is with us, made as we are out of the dust from the ground; the core of our lives, our spirits, are continually thirsty, and our very souls continually in need of the moisture that will give us life and make us life-bearing.

This elemental thirst is the theme of the story in John's gospel that recounts our Lord's encounter with a woman of Samaria at the well of Jacob. The woman came to the well to draw water; and the well provided what she came for. But, as Jesus in the gospel points out, "everyone who drinks of this water," the physical water of Jacob's well, "will thirst again." For the physical water that the woman came to draw from the well could never moisten the parched centre of her human spirit, or slake the deepmost thirst of her soul that made it necessary for her to come to the well again and again and again, whenever she needed to have some water to drink or to cook or wash with. So it was not the well that failed; it is just that the very dustiness of our human nature can never have its thirst finally slaked with any amount of physical water that is drawn up from a well or flows from the taps in our kitchens and bathrooms. Our bodies may be soaking wet, but our innermost spirits remain dry as dust, and our souls still thirst for the dew, the moisture that will make us whole and truly, eternally alive.

What Jesus promises is liberation from our dusty condition as creatures made out of the dust of the earth — and the liberation he promises also means eternal freedom from the thirst, the need that creatures of dust always have. For he speaks the truth and has power to bestow the Holy Spirit; and together, the divine Spirit and the truth that Jesus gives are like water, such water as "will become in [us] a spring of water welling up to eternal life." The springs will no longer be outside of us, but *in* us, perpetually irrigating our nature. And we who were made out of dust from the earth will be converted; we will cease to be dust and our spirits will become like true earth, our souls like rich soil capable of holding and nourishing the seeds that bear the fruit of life.

Indeed, we have already received this gift, for when we were baptized — when we were washed with the sign of water in the name of the Trinity — we received the Spirit and truth that Jesus alone can give. By our baptism God began the great reclamation of the dust we were made of; we have already started to become the new earth, rich, living, and life-bearing. And with this in view, God continues to sow in us the grain of heaven, which is the mystery of the body and blood of his only child Jesus Christ.

So, then, as God has begun the conversion of the dust that we are, let us be converted; let us take the grain, the life of the body and blood of Christ that God plants in the midst of our nature, and hold it, and nourish it, that Christ may yield fruit from this earth, and God may gather the harvest of his own glory out of the clay of our humanity.

THE WEDDING COVENANT

Then God spoke all these words:

I am the Lord your God, who brought you out of the land of Egypt, out of the house of slavery; you shall have no other gods before me.... For I the Lord your God am a jealous God, punishing children for the iniquity of parents, to the third and the fourth generation of those who reject me, but showing steadfast love to the thousandth generation of those who love me and keep my commandments.

(EXODUS 20:1–2, 5B–6)

The Christian religion is a lot like a wedding anniversary. We are always being asked to recall something that God did to unite us with himself, and to make it a cause for celebration, the way married couples invite us to remember the day they were united in wedlock and to make it the occasion for a party. But a wedding anniversary is an odd event. It is not really about that day, howsoever many years ago, when a man and a woman felt excitement, fright, extreme joy, and deep shock, all within the space of a few hours. No; a wedding anniversary is really about the way things are now. It is a chance for the husband and wife to renew the terms and conditions of their union, to refresh their commitment (in the words of the Prayer Book) to "perform and keep the vow and covenant betwixt them made."

And that is what the weekly anniversary of these Sundays in Lent is all about. Two Sundays ago we recalled the covenant that God made with Noah and his children; last Sunday we remembered the vow that God made to Abraham and his offspring; and today we heard the Ten Commandments, which are the terms and conditions of the covenant that God made with the children of Israel. So, just as a wedding anniversary allows a husband and wife to refresh "the vow and covenant betwixt them made," so our hearing of the Ten Commandments gives us a chance to renew the vow and covenant made betwixt God and ourselves.

The comparison between the Ten Commandments and wedding vows may seem far-fetched to you. For the Commandments are a matter of law, while wedding vows are supposed to be a matter of love. Or so we may have imagined. But stop for a minute, and think of the terms of the vow that husband and wife make to one another. Each partner promises "to have and to hold" the other "from this day forward; for better, for worse, for richer, for poorer, in sickness and in health, to love and to cherish, till death do us part." This is just what God promises to his people when he utters the Commandments — but without the condition, "till death do us part." The Ten Commandments are the wedding covenant between God and his people, by which God vows "to have and to hold" us "for better for worse, for richer for poorer, in sickness and in health, to love and to cherish," even "to the thousandth generation of those who love me and keep my commandments." But that is as good as saying forever; for who can imagine a thousand generations? So the vow and covenant made betwixt God and his people can never come to an end.

Of course, the Ten Commandments are a good deal more specific than the wedding vow, in the terms they set for the union betwixt God and his people. But the purpose is the same. As in the wedding vow a woman and a man "plight their troth," that is, promise to keep faith with one another, so in the Ten Commandments God and his people plight their troth with one another. On these terms and conditions God will keep faith with them as his only chosen people, and they will keep faith with the Lord as their only God.

But the terms and conditions of God's covenant with his people are not all one way; and this is where the comparison of the Commandments with wedding vows begins to break down. For we are required not only to have "no other gods before us," to love the Lord our God, and him only, with all our heart and with all our soul and with all our mind and with all our strength. We are also required to keep faith with our neighbours — indeed, to love our neighbours as ourselves. We must give a day of rest and freedom to our spouses, to our children, to our animals, to the strangers who moved in next door, and yes, even to ourselves; we must honour our parents; we must not commit murder, or adultery, or theft, or perjury against anybody who dwells among us, whether related to us or not, whether a member of this church or not, whether we like them or not. God has shared his life with us, and given us all the good things that we enjoy; and God calls us to support each other in sharing that same life of his, and to make sure that each may be secure in enjoying the good things that God has given them. In short, we cannot keep faith with God unless we keep faith with our neighbours.

But if we cannot keep faith with God unless we keep faith with our neighbours, neither can we truly keep faith with our neighbours unless we keep faith with God. This is the other basic point of the Commandments; a point that, though basic, is often harder for us to accept. For we may think that we get along well enough with folks around us, without bringing God into the matter. Indeed, we probably think that we get along with our neighbours as well as we do because we do *not* bring God into the matter. Religion, we think, makes for bad feeling; so best leave it to one side, and just be neighbourly.

Now, practical as such an attitude might sound, it really does not work. It is rather like trying to rattle around in your house without bringing your spouse into the matter, or whoever else shares the house with you. That other person makes it possible for you to do everything else; just so, it is God who makes it possible for you to be neighbourly — who made it possible for your parents to be neighbourly and to teach you neighbourliness. For that is part of the vow and covenant that God has made betwixt himself and us, his people: that he should give us grace to be as gracious as he commands us to be, and that he should be our God especially in making us the people he desires to have.

So the Ten Commandments are the vow and covenant made betwixt God and ourselves; and though they may seem every bit as fearsome as the vow and covenant made between a husband and wife at their wedding, yet living them is proof of the love that made God plight his troth to us and made us plight our troth to him. He will never leave us nor forsake us, but will show steadfast love, even to the thousandth generation of those who love him and keep his commandments, the vow and covenant betwixt us made.

TEMPLES

Jesus answered them, "Destroy this temple, and in three days I will raise it up." The Jews then said, "This temple has been under construction for forty-six years, and will you raise it up in three days?" But he was speaking of the temple of his body.

(JOHN 2:19–21)

Jesus was always getting into arguments. We like to dress up those occasions of "mutual disagreement" and call them controversies. But arguments are what they were. This is not a recommendation that we all go out and argue with anybody we meet, nor should we take the fact that Jesus got into arguments as blanket permission for us to be unpleasant whenever we feel like it. For Jesus did not get into arguments on a whim. His arguments were always a matter of bearing witness to some important truth — some portion of the truth about God that the establishment and its spokesmen were unwilling to hear.

And so Jesus took offence at the buying and selling that was going on in the outer courtyard of the temple in Jerusalem. Having taken offence, he took it upon himself to drive the vendors, entrepreneurs, and hucksters out of the house of God his Father. That is when some official spokesmen showed up and said, "Show us your authority for making such a mess here." And "Jesus answered them, 'Destroy this temple, and in three days I will raise it up.' The Jews then said, 'This temple has been under construction for forty-six years, and will you raise it up in three days?' But Jesus was speaking of the temple of his body."

This is one of those moments in John's gospel when our Lord plays with his antagonists — he makes fools of them, without their realizing it. For he and they were standing right in the middle of the temple. So when Jesus spoke of the destruction and raising up of the temple, the officials naturally thought he was talking about the building round about them, the temple that King Herod had begun to renovate and rebuild some forty-six years earlier. Then St. John lets us in on the secret, the joke: Jesus actually meant "the temple of his own body." Jesus was saying: Kill me, destroy my life, and I will raise it up again in three days — that is my authority, the proof of my authority.

At the same time, Jesus' response to the officials implies an awesome claim about his own person — and about the building in which he and his antagonists were standing. The temple in Jerusalem was supposed to be the Almighty's dwelling-place, the only house on earth of the one true God. By identifying his own body as "this temple," the Jesus of John's gospel was suggesting that he himself was the place where God dwells — and that God did not dwell, or no longer dwelled, in the temple building. His own body was the sacred space, and wherever he was, there God was.

Here we have a matter that has been much exercising our bishops and their advisers — the connection between Christ, the people of Christ, and church-buildings. Our leaders have a sense that too many Anglicans are obsessive about their churches — if you like, their temples — and allow the upkeep and beautification of the physical plant to absorb too much of their parish budgets and energies. "We should be worshipping God, not buildings!" these voices cry; "We should be serving people, not architecture!"

The bishops have a point, a serious point. Unfortunately, it is also a point that strikes this particular church right where it lives. For as a parish we have committed ourselves to just the sort of building program that the bishops appear to have called into question. We are renovating the basement in order to expand the useable space in our physical plant. In the light of what our bishops have been saying, shouldn't we stop and ask ourselves whether we have got our priorities straight?

Well, as Anglicans we acknowledge that it sometimes useful to listen to what bishops say; and as Christians, it is even more important to act as prophets and ask one another whether we have truly heard the gospel. But I am willing to argue that we have not gone wrong in devoting so much money and so much energy to the renovation of this building, which is both God's house and our house.

We need to take seriously Jesus' words that his own body is a temple. His words can be matched with a rhetorical question that St. Paul once addressed to the Corinthians: "Do you not know that you are God's temple and that God's Spirit dwells in you?" (1 Corinthians 3:16). We ourselves are the house of God — not just our souls, the immaterial, spiritual part of us, but the whole of our lives as persons, which means our bodies as well as our souls. That is why, when we pray, it is not good enough for us merely to adopt a religious frame of mind and think prayerfully. We also need to pray with our bodies — to kneel or to stand — and to bow toward the altar "as the greatest place of God's residence on earth." For we take ourselves bound to worship with body as well as in soul whenever we come where God is worshipped.

But bodies, being bodies, are frail things. They need shelter. Our forebears built this house to the honour and glory of almighty God, and we have kept it up, kept it clean and in excellent repair for the same reason. But still, *God* needs no shelter — it is *we*, our bodies, that need the shelter. And so, if this building is a sacrament of God — an outward and visible sign of the inward and spiritual presence of the Lord — it is also a sacrament of this community, an outward and visible sign of the persons, the lives, who gather together to worship God with their bodies as well as in their souls.

So, no, we should not worship our church-building, nor should we let architecture take control of our duty to see and care for the needs of people. But we also have a duty to be seen, to be seen as God's people in this spot, at this very intersection of thoroughfares and roads in a city where many have come to dwell; and this building is the best way to do so — for starters. For this temple is not the end of the sacrament we celebrate within its walls; it is simply the point where the sacrament that is this community takes its weekly start; and having received the body of Christ, we as a community begin again to *be* the body of Christ in the world, here at one particular corner among the many corners and intersections of the world.

NAMING GOD

But Moses said to God, "If I come to the Israelites and say to them, 'The God of your ancestors has sent me to you,' and they ask me, 'What is his name?' what shall I say to them?" God said to Moses, "I AM WHO I AM." He said further, "Thus you shall say to the Israelites, 'I AM has sent me to you.' " God also said to Moses, "Thus you shall say to the Israelites, 'The Lord, the God of your ancestors, the God of Abraham, the God of Isaac, and the God of Jacob, has sent me to you': This is my name forever, and this my title for all generations."

(EXODUS 3:13–15)

I sometimes wonder whether we do not use the word "God" too much, especially when we say our prayers. I am certainly in favour of praying, of addressing and listening to the God who addresses and listens to us through Jesus Christ, in the power of the Holy Spirit. I just wonder whether we go about it in the right way — whether we need to begin so very many of our prayers with the address, "O God." For the word *god* is a generic title, not a proper name. It tells us *what* the Almighty is, but it does not tell us *who* the Almighty is. That may sound like an odd thing to say — odd, because we are so accustomed to thinking that there is only one God, the Christian god, that we take it for granted that "God" is this God's proper name. To whom else would we be talking?

As it happens, this is the very question that arose in the story of the calling of Moses — how he was minding his father-in-law's sheep in the wilderness when he caught sight of a bush all ablaze with fire yet unconsumed by the flames; how he turned aside, and found himself addressed by "the God of your father, the God of Abraham, the God of Isaac, and the God of Jacob." This God told Moses that he had been chosen to bring his own people, the Hebrews, out of slavery in Egypt. And Moses responded by asking a question: "If I come to the Israelites and say to them, 'The God of your ancestors has sent me to you,' and they ask me, 'What is his name?' — what shall I say to them?" It was a good question. For Moses and the Israelites lived in a world where many gods were worshipped and adored; and each one of these gods had a proper name, like Isis and Zeus, Marduk and Artemis. So Moses was not out of line when he asked the God who addressed him out of the burning bush, "What is your proper name?"

God replied and said to Moses, "I AM WHO I AM. Thus you shall say to the Israelites, 'I AM has sent me to you.' " This answer has all the earmarks of a proper name; and indeed, both Judaism and Christianity have always treated it as such. In Hebrew, God's name is spelled with four letters — YHWH; letters that Christian writers transmuted into the word "Jehovah." As it happens, that is only a guess; nobody knows for sure how the original Hebrew word was really pronounced because those who transcribed the Hebrew text of Scripture always left out the vowels. YHWH is like the name "Philip" without the *i*'s, or like the name "Edna" without the letters *E* and *a*. The Hebrew scribes were not being careless; they omitted the vowels of God's name quite deliberately, because Jewish tradition decreed that the name of God was too holy for humans to speak it. So, wherever the four letters YHWH appeared, the Hebrew scribes inserted vowel markings that indicated that another word should be substituted, the word *Adonai*, which is translated in English as "Lord." That is how we come to address the Almighty as "the Lord God"; and by this title we mean, "the God who is I AM."

Thus it appears that the Most High does indeed have a proper name — only, the name itself is so holy, that mere mortals must never presume to speak it. Although we are privileged to know God's proper name, yet we know it as the name that we must keep secret even from ourselves.

When you think about it, the secret is not very hard to keep because, as names go, the name that God revealed to Moses does not tell us very much. Each one of us can say, "I am," but whomever we are speaking to will naturally expect us to complete the sentence, for instance, "I am ... Stephen Reynolds." But not this God. This God never completes the sentence. On the contrary, the God of the burning bush answered Moses by refusing to give him any direct answer at all. For the real import of the Almighty's response to Moses was this: "I AM ... WHO I AM. That's all you need to know, that's all the Israelites need to know: *I AM*." It is as if the Lord God were saying, "My name is none of your business!"

We seem to be left in a quandary: the more we know of God through prayer, the more our knowledge seems to be stymied. It is as if God reveals himself with one hand and empties the revelation of all content with the other. When we speak with God, we know whom we are addressing, but cannot fix a definite proper name upon him. No wonder so many saints have sometimes felt as if they were praying into a black hole; no wonder we try to fill the gap, or at least put a title to our ignorance, by treating the generic word God as if it were the real proper name of the one who told Moses, "I AM WHO I AM."

What shall we say to this? Is the Almighty only fooling around with us, only luring us into intimacy and then leaving us in the lurch? The story of Moses' calling seems to be repeated in the life of everyone who takes prayer seriously. The Most High tantalized Moses with a bush that was ablaze but did not burn up, and then, having caught his attention, refused to give a straight answer to the straight question, "What is your name?" The God who loves us seems to turn coy when we respond with loving prayer, and appears to retreat from us when we try to seal our prayers by naming the intimate name of the divine suitor. So we settle on the name "God," a name that says everything in general and nothing in particular; and we use this generic name with frustration, because love is nothing if not particular.

But the God who refuses to be named like the idols of the nations, who will not be captured in a word with vowels as well as consonants, this same God nevertheless gives us something else by which to know and name his love. At the conclusion of the story of Moses' calling, the God of the burning bush tells Moses: "Thus you shall say to the Israelites, 'The Lord, the God of your ancestors, the God of Abraham, the God of Isaac, and the God of Jacob, has sent me to you.' This is my name for ever, and this is my title for all generations." The name of God is I AM, yes — but here we find out the completion of the sentence. YHWH, the great I AM, is I AM FAITHFUL TO ABRAHAM, ISAAC, AND JACOB. It is as if God's proper name were not a word but a story, the story of his faithfulness to particular people. And the story does not end with Abraham, or with his son Isaac, or with his grandson Jacob; it continues down to Moses and his own generation, and far, far beyond, to Deborah the judge and Hannah the mother of Samuel, to David the king and Jeremiah the prophet, to Judah the Maccabee and the mother who perished with her seven sons rather than betray the covenant, to Anne, the mother of Mary, to Zechariah and Elizabeth, the parents of John the Baptist, and to Mary, the mother of our Lord Jesus Christ. This is our God, the God whose name is the story of faithfulness to particular people for the sake of his covenant with Israel; the God whose faithfulness was, in the fullness of time, made flesh in Jesus Christ.

And the story that is the name of God continues, not only in the broad sweep of cosmic history, but also in the joys and pains, in the griefs and in the graciousness that each one of us experiences from day to day. As the saying goes, God is in the details; and perhaps God can only be named, truly named, when we have learned how to tell the story of I AM — the story of the God who is I AM FAITHFUL TO ABRAHAM, ISAAC, AND JACOB, TO MOSES AND DAVID AND JEREMIAH, TO PETER AND PAUL AND ONESIMUS — AND TO YOU. This is where prayer begins — not with the ascription of a generic title, but with the telling of a story through Jesus Christ, with the willingness to say who this God is by recounting what this God has done for us, in us, and with us in particular. Then we shall be able to take the secret name upon our lips and speak the vowels as well as the consonants of the Lord God, the God who is I AM.

SIGHT

1 Samuel 16:1–13
John 9:1–3, 39–41

God decides that King Saul has not worked out and needs to be replaced. So the Lord tells the prophet Samuel to visit a man named Jesse, who lives at Bethlehem, for God has made up his mind that one of Jesse's sons should take Saul's place as king. So Samuel goes to Bethlehem and arranges to meet Jesse and his sons. The eldest of the boys is Eliab, and he is, quite frankly, a hunk — muscular, tall, and drop-dead gorgeous. Wow! says Samuel, look at this guy — he's got to be the one. But then Samuel receives an insight from God: "Do not look on his appearance or on the height of his stature, because I have rejected him; for the Lord does not see as mortals see; they look on the outward appearance, but the Lord looks on the heart." Samuel blinks his eyes, and shrugs. This job of king-making will not be the piece of cake he thought it would be. And so it proves. Jesse has nine of his sons stand before Samuel, and not one of them registers even so much as a rustle or squeak in that innermost ear by which Samuel hears the word of God. Samuel begins to wonder if he had got the address right: Did the Lord really say *Jesse* of Bethlehem? Samuel knows his hearing is not what it used to be, so maybe the Lord said, Go to *Joshua* of Bethlehem. Because look at these nine sons of Jesse, each one drop-dead gorgeous — and the Lord hasn't chosen any of them. Samuel sighs, then decides to take one last crack at it. He says to Jesse, "Are all your sons here?" And Jesse replies, "No, there's my youngest kid, but he's out keeping the sheep." So Samuel figures, in for a penny, in for a pound, and tells Jesse to send for the boy. Eventually this youngest son arrives on the scene; it is David. "Now he was ruddy, and had beautiful eyes, and was handsome" — in other words, just as much of a hunk as his older brothers. And "the Lord said to Samuel, 'Rise and anoint him; for this is the one.' "

In other words, the Lord God gets to eat his cake and have it too. He announces that he does not make decisions the way humans do, by the standards of physical beauty or strength: "The Lord does not see as mortals see; they look on the outward appearance, but the Lord looks on the heart." But in the end, the Lord chooses David — who, we gather, happens to have the right stuff in his heart; but he also happens to be good-looking. As far as the Lord is concerned, it is a win-win situation — great heart *plus* drop-dead good looks. Central casting at the divine studio has done it again.

But perhaps I am missing the most important point of all. In the world of Samuel, Jesse, and David, the eldest son was the son that mattered; he came first in everything, and he got the lion's share of his father's property. All other sons were (so to speak) back-up copies, useful but not essential. And you notice that the youngest of Jesse's sons, David, was not with the rest of the sons when Samuel arrived; he was out doing chores, while Jesse and his older boys feasted with the prophet. So the fact that David happened to be handsome was, in a manner of speaking, God's concession to human prejudice, not the reason why God chose David. No, in choosing David, the youngest son, to be the next king of Israel, God really did turn human standards on their head.

Still, the story of Samuel's search for the new king of Israel highlights a habit so common, so universal, so reflexive that it must be a built-in feature of human nature. And that is the habit of making beauty or blemish a moral issue. We take it for granted that the beautiful person must be good, until proven otherwise; and likewise, if we see someone who is blemished in some way, perhaps even ugly, we assume that there is something bad about them. The words that the Lord spoke to Samuel are true: "Mortals look on the outward appearance."

We have an extreme confirmation of this human habit in John's gospel. One day, "as Jesus walked along, he saw a man blind from birth. His disciples asked him, 'Rabbi, who sinned, this man or his parents, that he was born blind?' " The question reveals a lot not only about the disciples but also about human attitudes in general. For the question the disciples asked works on the assumption that a physical blemish or handicap such as blindness must be punishment — well-deserved punishment — for something done wrong, for a sin committed in the past.

But Jesus has no truck with such sentiments, nor with the moral value we place on outward beauty and outward blemishes, that the physically beautiful must be thoroughly good and that the physically blemished must be inwardly disfigured. For when the disciples wondered whose sin caused the man to be born blind, Jesus answered, "Neither this man nor his parents sinned; he was born blind so that God's works might be revealed in him." Now we may have some trouble grappling with the idea that one particular person should have been born blind in order that God might work a miracle at a later point. But the first thing Jesus said is the really startling point: the blind man's blindness is not the result of a moral fault, nor is it a sign of sin. It is just a fact of life, to be dealt with on that basis — with kindness, with consideration, with due attention to the handicapped person's needs.

But of course there is the second part of Jesus' answer to the disciples — that the blind man they had just seen "was born blind so that God's works might be revealed in him." Here Jesus is acting much as God acted in the household of Jesse. Then the Lord told Samuel, "The Lord does not see as mortals see; they look on the outward appearance, but the Lord looks on the heart." Now the Lord Jesus does the same thing: he who "knew what was in everyone" looked not on the outward appearance of this one blind man but on this one man's heart. And looking on this particular person's heart, he saw something of what the Lord God saw in David — a heart ready to have faith and to be faithful; a heart that could see the truth of God, even though his eyes were sightless. That is the point of Jesus' remark about the man having been born blind "so that God's works might be revealed in him." In a sense, his whole life had been a preparation for his encounter with Jesus; and as we learn in the rest of the story, the man lived up to that preparation. He was harassed, insulted, sneered at by the authorities; but he remained unshakeable in his commitment to Jesus. And so at the very end of the story Jesus takes an opportunity to drive the point home. "Jesus said, 'I came into this world for judgement so that those who do not see may see, and those who do see may become blind.' Some of the Pharisees near him heard this and said to him, 'Surely we are not blind, are we?' Jesus said to them, 'If you were blind, you would not have sin. But now that you say, "We see," your sin remains.' " Those Pharisees had twenty-twenty vision with their physical eyesight; but they were blind when it came to *in*sight, to the sort of vision that looks on the heart and sees into the inner and true worth of a person — be it a man blind from birth or Jesus of Nazareth.

Now we are called to this same sort of insight, to see no longer as mere mortals see but to see as the Lord sees. And that is not something that we can pick up by consulting self-help manuals. Because it is a matter of seeing as God sees, this insight is a gift of God. But God spoils us, you know; the Lord bestows this gift, if only we will pray for it. And if we pray the Lord for this gift of insight, we shall have it from the Lord. Then we shall be able to look on the hearts of all whom we meet, and judge them truly, without prejudice and in real charity, because we shall be seeing them as the Lord sees both them and ourselves.

GOD'S SPITTLE

Jesus spat on the ground and with the spittle made a bit of clay, then anointed the eyes of the man blind from birth. So much for the safe solemnity that lets us think that Jesus is the embodiment of middle-class values raised to the infinite power, and the gospel a matter of high-minded precepts for the soul alone. Spittle is *not nice* — and what could be more disgusting than to spit on the ground, make the clay with the spittle, and then rub it on someone else's eyes? But this same action of our Lord, offensive as it might seem, this same action is the heart of the gospel.

First, consider who it was that spat on the ground. It was Jesus. More than that, it was the Jesus of John's gospel, the Jesus whose ministry and actions on earth are seen from the other side of the resurrection, in the light of the divine power that was to be manifested in the risen Lord. That divine power is creative, for the resurrection was the definitive act of new creation. Just as God brought all things into being out of nothing, so God brought the crucified Jesus into new being out of life's utter negation, death.

Next, consider what this Jesus did when he spat on the ground. With his spittle, with the moisture of his mouth, he made some clay. Think back to the Bible's story of how God created the first human being. In the book of Genesis it says that "the Lord God formed man from the dust of the ground."

How did God form this being from the dust of the ground? Well, the first human's name was Adam; and in Hebrew the name "Adam" is akin to the word for "earth," in particular, the clay-like earth that you find in a field after a good spring rain, the clay-like earth that is good for farming. With the dew of the Spirit, the Lord God made just such a clay out of the dust of the ground and formed the first human, Adam, a creature of good moist earth. And so, Jesus, who was the power of God's new creation, made clay out of his spittle. The Lord joined the dew of his mouth with the dust of the ground, and formed a sacrament of the new Adam. For that is just what this clay was, a sacrament, an outward and visible sign of the new Adam.

Finally, what did the new Adam do with this sacrament of clay? He daubed or rubbed it on the eyes of the man born blind, so that the man might see — and, seeing, might know and believe in Jesus, the Son of God. Do you yourselves now see the importance of what Jesus did? I myself have only just begun to: I glimpse the connection, and it hurts my eyes, because I myself am still learning to see, that is, to see with faith. Jesus spat on the ground and made clay out of the spittle: the Father sent Jesus to be made one with the dust of the ground that we humans are, so that he might be applied to our blindness — so that he might anoint our condition and heal us. What are we to do with the new sight that he has given us? We must confess him and seek him out, as did the man in the gospel who had been healed of his blindness; we must seek Jesus out, in order that we may believe in him and give him worship; in order that we may train our new vision on him and let our whole being become the new Adam, the new clay formed in baptism from the dew of God's Spirit and the grace of the Son of God's humanity.

THE WAYS OF GOD

The Lord does not see as mortals see; they look on the outward appearance, but the Lord looks on the heart.

(1 SAMUEL 16:6–7)

I came into this world for judgement so that those who do not see may see, and those who do see may become blind.

(JOHN 9:39)

Some thirty-seven years ago, lying awake in the dead of a stifling July night, I decided to become a genius. You know, one of the mighty minds of the twentieth century, a nabob of the intellect; a veritable Einstein, a breath-taking Picasso, a luminous Beethoven, a stirring Shakespeare, all in one. The trouble was, I was rotten at math, hopeless at algebra, totally clueless about physics; couldn't draw or paint to save my life; and didn't know whether a page of music was upside-down or right-side-up. So I figured that I had some catching-up to do.

One of the first projects that I decided upon was to read the entire canon of English literature that summer, from *Beowulf* through T. S. Eliot and Virginia Woolf. *Beowulf* was a challenge until I discovered that it had been translated into modern English; in the meantime, I had discovered a rather different challenge in the form of *Paradise Lost*, John Milton's epic poem in twelve books. I read Milton's opening prayer, in which he invoked God's "aid to my advent'rous song,"

while it pursues
Things unattempted yet in prose or rhyme.
And chiefly thou, O Spirit, that dost prefer
Before all temples th' upright heart and pure,
Instruct me ... What in me is dark
Illumine; what is low, raise and support;
That to the height of this great argument
I may assert eternal Providence,
And justify the ways of God to men.[1]

(*PARADISE LOST*, BOOK I:13–19, 22–26)

"Yep," I said to my thirteen-year-old self, "that's what I'm going to do when I grow up: I'll 'justify the ways of God to men' — and just for good measure, to women too." Although I never did become a genius, the funny thing is, when I grew up, justifying the ways of God is precisely what I ended up doing — and am still trying to do to this day.

It has not always been easy. In fact, it has *never* been easy. This is not because God's ways are utterly unintelligible to the human mind, or absolutely impenetrable to the human heart. The reason for the difficulty lies in something else. In this, as in so much else, dear St. Augustine got as close to putting his finger on the matter as any. He once said: "Since it is God we are speaking of, you do not comprehend it. If you could comprehend it, it would not be God."[1] This is not a permission-slip for the cheap mysticism that masquerades its mental sloth and, still more, its spiritual vacuity as a higher form of religious experience. On the contrary, Augustine's remark was meant to invite the faithful to an infinite adventure, a ceaseless exploration

---

1.   Augustine, *Sermon* 117, § 5.

not only of God's ways but also of God's very life itself. And once you have discovered something of God and God's ways, you also discover that there is more — infinitely more — still to be discovered.

So the road of understanding is long, and lengths of it will feel very arduous indeed. One accepts the sweaty passages, just as one rejoices in the stretches of fun. There are times, though, when something makes justifying God's ways very much harder than seems quite fair. It is not always a shocking event, a tragedy, or a bitter setback. Sometimes it is merely a text of Scripture. And today's gospel is one of them. "As Jesus walked along," it tells us, "he saw a man blind from birth. His disciples asked him, 'Rabbi, who sinned, this man or his parents, that he was born blind?' Jesus answered, 'Neither this man nor his parents sinned; he was born blind so that God's works might be revealed in him.' " This saying starts off promisingly: Jesus goes against the grain of religious reflex and repudiates the notion that a handicap such as blindness or an illness is punishment for sin. But then he maintains that the man was born blind for a purpose — "so that God's works might be revealed in him." It sounds as if it is God's way to inflict suffering on an individual human and then, one day many years later, to heal him, pouf! just like that! — thereby razzle-dazzling the rubes and turning the man himself into a poster-boy for providence.

So, then, Mr. Theologian in Residence, justify *that*, if you can.

Let's return to the beginning of the story, to the question that the disciples asked of Jesus: "Rabbi, who sinned, this man or his parents, that he was born blind?" In ancient Judaism — and, let's be honest, in common, garden-variety Christianity to this day, as well — anybody with a handicap was ostracized because people assumed that God himself had ostracized that person. In this mentality, it goes without saying that an illness or a handicap is evil; but evil things are supposed to happen only to evil people; therefore, these afflicted persons must be suffering condign punishment for sins against God committed either by themselves, or by their parents, or by one of their remote ancestors. In other words, it is a matter of blaming the victim on system.

Jesus, as I say, repudiated this view. But what does he mean when he says that "this man … was born blind so that God's works might be revealed in him"? Does he mean that God deliberately caused the man to be blind, with a view to giving him the gift of sight at some later date? Well, no; that is not what Jesus says. He makes no mention of God having a hand in the man's blindness. "This man," it says, "*was born* blind." The verb is passive, not active — which implies that afflictions happen, cannot be avoided, in a world out of whack in itself because it is out of sync with God. For that very reason, God's works are always works of healing and making whole — in short, works of salvation.

But if the world is out of sync with God, and therefore out of whack in itself, what of "the world rulers of this present age"? Here we are talking not only about monarchs and mullahs, presidents and prime ministers but also about figures lower down on the food chain of power, the enforcers of a community's standards, society's self-appointed gate-keepers and guardians, like the Pharisees of today's story. They held no office and possessed no jurisdiction; their only authority was their zeal to maintain the values of their religion, which (they believed) were the same as the values of their society. So they took it upon themselves to interrogate the man healed of blindness and, because he would not knuckle under and submit to them, they enforced the view that Jesus had repudiated: " 'You were born entirely in sins,' [they said] … "*And they drove him out.*" Once shunned because of his blindness, he — now sighted — is again ostracized for claiming to have seen what the gate-keepers do not see.

Here we begin to glimpse the theme of today's readings as a whole — the contrast between seeing and not seeing, between human judgement and God's vision. In the first reading, Samuel went up to Bethlehem to anoint one of Jesse's sons as king of Israel in place of Saul. Samuel "looked on Eliab," the eldest of Jesse's boys, obviously a tall, well-toned, gorgeous hunk; "and [Samuel] thought, 'Surely the Lord's anointed is now before the Lord.' But the Lord said to Samuel, 'Do not look on his appearance or on the height of his stature, because I have rejected him; for the Lord does not see as mortals see; they look on the outward appearance, but the Lord looks on the heart.' "

The Lord does not see as mortals see; they look on the outward appearance, but the Lord looks on the heart. Hold this saying in your minds, and return with me to the gospel. After the Pharisees had driven out the man healed of his blindness, Jesus sought him out and revealed to him that even at that moment he was speaking with the Messiah of God, the Saviour and Redeemer of the world. The man "said, 'Lord, I believe.' And he worshipped [Jesus]." Then Jesus drove the point home: "I came into this world for judgement so that those who do not see may see, and those who do see may become blind." Some of the Pharisees near him overheard this remark and said to him, 'Surely we are not blind, are we?' " And Jesus replied: "If you were blind, you would not have sin. But now that you say, 'We see,' your sin remains." *The Lord does not see as mortals see; they look on the outward appearance, but the Lord looks on the heart.*

Since the world is out of sync with God, and therefore out

of whack in itself, anybody who makes appearances the measure by which they judge things is working with a faulty standard and thus making false assessments. And the irony does not stop there. "The Lord looks on the heart," on the inside; and so are we called to do. Which means that if we do not seek to look on the heart of things, on the inside of reality, we shall make mistakes about the very outward appearances that we can see. Those Pharisees could see very well that a man born blind now had sight; but the glare of their own standards — standards that, by the way, served to give them power over their neighbours — these very standards blinded them, handicapped, disabled them when it came to looking on the heart of what they had seen. The witness of today's gospel, then, is that those who hold power in the world and use it to exclude others are playing a fool's game, for they are in fact condoning, using, and benefiting from what is wrong with the world, namely, its alienation from God. As St. Paul said in a reading that we heard a few Sundays ago: "God chose what is foolish in the world to shame the wise; God chose what is weak in the world to shame the strong;" — God chose those in the world who are blind to shame the sighted; — "God chose what is low and despised in the world, even things that are not, to reduce to nothing things that are, so that no one might boast in the presence of God" (1 Corinthians 1:27–29). Insofar as the powers-that-be, the gatekeepers and guardians of society's values, use religion to shore up and sanction their exclusion and oppression of the widow and orphan, the stranger, the hungry, the homeless poor, the blind, and the lame in their midst, they "boast in the presence of God" — and to no end but their own exclusion, for they have made piety a perversion.

There, but for the grace of God, go we; and perhaps I myself should not regret too keenly God's decision not to let me become a genius, insofar as genius is a form of worldly power and therefore liable to corruption. None of us can boast in the presence of God, so long as the homeless poor are without shelter, the naked remain unclothed, the refugee cannot yet return home, and the wounded heart has no hope and is without God in the world. It is the providence of God to dwell with those who know that they "see in a mirror, dimly," and long passionately to "see face to face"; who know that they "know only in part;" and ache with desire to "know fully, even as [they] have been fully known" (1 Corinthians 13:12); who love and delight in the God whom they do not comprehend, so that they may understand and justify the ways of God.

Not John Milton but another poet, and a better theologian, put it this way:

> We shall not cease from exploration
> And the end of all our exploring
> Will be to arrive where we started
> And know the place for the first time.

> (T. S. ELIOT, *FOUR QUARTETS*, "LITTLE GIDDING," V)

The funny thing is, each time we arrive where we started and know the place for the first time — each time we have found a stopping-place on which to "justify the ways of God to men" and women — we shall find that it is not a place to settle in but merely a temporary anchorage, from which we must sooner or later adventure forth again, to explore the infinite depths of God.

FIRST SIGNS

The hand of the Lord came upon me, and he brought me out by the spirit of the Lord and set me down in the middle of a valley; it was full of bones. He led me all around them; there were very many lying in the valley, and they were very dry. He said to me, "Mortal, can these bones live?" I answered, "O Lord God, you know."

(EZEKIEL 37:1–3)

Jesus said to her, "Your brother will rise again." Martha said to him, "I know that he will rise again in the resurrection on the last day." Jesus said to her, "I am the resurrection and the life. Those who believe in me, even though they die, will live, and everyone who lives and believes in me will never die. Do you believe this?"

(JOHN 11:23–26)

S ome years, even when the calendar tells us that spring has come, all we see around us are signs of winter — winter, winter everywhere. It's not fair! Perhaps that is why, at our house, a few rows of little brown and white cups assume such importance. These cups are filled with earth, and from this earth in each little cup seedlings begin to sprout. The cups are sprayed with water every day, and every day they are moved from one bedroom to the next to catch the best sunlight. For these little seedlings in their little cups are the first shoots of spring, and the first signs that there is indeed life after winter.

Something of the same is true about today's readings. They obviously point toward the great and mighty wonder we shall be celebrating on Easter Day, namely, the resurrection. The first reading came from the book of the prophet Ezekiel, and recorded a vision that the Lord God granted the prophet — a vision of Israel and Judah once defeated and scattered by war, re-created and brought together again by the this same Lord God. And in today's gospel we heard the story of the raising of Lazarus — an advance shoot of the resurrection if ever there was one.

But the raising of Lazarus was not a resurrection. It was the resuscitation of a corpse. It is indeed but a shoot of resurrection, not the full-grown truth of resurrection; it is but a first sign of Easter Day, not Easter Day itself. For the resurrection is not just the resuscitation of a corpse, as in the case of Lazarus; nor is it only the reconstruction of a community, as in the vision seen by Ezekiel.

In today's collect we ask God to "breathe upon us with the power of your Spirit, that we may be raised to new life in Christ." The emphasis here is on the word *new*. When Lazarus was brought out of the tomb, he certainly received "new life" — but in the sense of a second chance at life. Otherwise, he was exactly the same as before his illness and death, and the gospel strongly hints that he would die again. Resurrection means something else — not just a second chance at life, but a real change in how one is alive; such a change, that one cannot die again, ever. When Jesus was raised from the dead, he was not a resuscitated corpse; he was no longer exactly the same as before his crucifixion. He had undergone a real change; and though he was certainly the same person, he had become very different — and in that difference lay the newness of risen life.

In another part of the gospel, Jesus is reported as saying:

"Unless a grain of wheat falls into the earth and dies, it remains just a single grain; but if it dies, it bears much fruit" (John 12:24). When a seed is planted in the ground and begins to sprout, it does (in a certain sense) die. It ceases to be what it was; it becomes something more and even different from what it was — something that you would never have expected it to become, if you looked at it sitting in the palm of your hand. And so it was with Jesus himself. He died and was buried in the ground. But then his life became like a grain of wheat: it began to change, the way a sprouting seed breaks its former shell and sends forth shoots that will have a wholly new, a wholly different appearance. The destruction of Jesus' life on the cross, and the breaking-open of his body in the grave, thus bore the fruit of new life; life so thoroughly new, that none of his persecutors, nor even any of his own disciples, were able to imagine it while they had him in the palm of their hand.

And that problem continues to this very day; we are, as St. Paul says, "of the earth, earthy," and so our imaginations keep looking for signs of life on the ground instead of shoots from heaven. God knows that; and so the divine word seeks to astonish us with earthy happenings and events on ground level, that we may learn to look higher. Such is the point of today's gospel and its account of the resuscitation of Lazarus after four days in the tomb. They are about earthy events that seem unimaginable until they happen; they are meant to make us wonder, and the wonder we feel is as much a first shoot of resurrection, a first sign of Easter, as those little seedlings in their little cups in the rectory are the first shoots, the first signs of spring. They are not the mature fruit, whose beauty will bear no resemblance to the original seed; but they are indications that the beauty of the flower is on its way; and for that we may rejoice. In the same way, the gospel of Lazarus's resuscitation is an indication that the resurrection is indeed on its way. In the time that remains to us until Easter, perhaps our first duty as believers is to allow ourselves to wonder and be amazed; for our amazement at the resuscitation of Lazarus will make us ready to rejoice truly, and with faith, at the resurrection of Jesus.

ACCORDING TO THE ORDER
OF MELCHIZEDEK

*So also Christ did not glorify himself in becoming a high
priest, but was appointed by the one who said to him,
"You are my Son,
today I have begotten you";
as he says also in another place,
"You are a priest for ever,
according to the order of Melchizedek."
Although he was a Son, he learned obedience through what
he suffered; and having been made perfect, he became the
source of eternal salvation for all who obey him, having
been designated by God a high priest according to the order
of Melchizedek.*

(HEBREWS 5:5–6, 8–10)

WE ARE nearing the heart of the Christian year, and of
the whole Christian gospel too. Holy Week is almost
upon us, the week when we shall begin to follow the passage of
Jesus from triumph at the gates of Jerusalem, through betrayal,
punishment, death, and finally resurrection. But even before
we get to Holy Week, to the heart of the gospel and the Christian year, we can feel its beat get stronger as the Church begins
to probe the meaning of it all — not only what happened to
Jesus, but also what he was about and who he was.

For this very reason the Church calls us to ruminate a passage from the Letter to the Hebrews. It is a short passage, only five verses long; but it fooled our notion that keeping it short keeps it simple. The truth of the matter is, that this short reading manages to pack a lot of baggage into its five verses, and some of that baggage is so peculiar to us that we cannot understand why the author thought to pack it at all. Indeed, the whole passage turns on one image that may be so very obscure as to be meaningless to us. It is the image of Jesus as "a high priest according to the order of Melchizedek."

Melchizedek? Who is he? Or is it *she?* Or is Melchizedek a *what?* The reading twice refers to "the order of Melchizedek," and for all we know, that could be like the Order of Canada or the Order of the British Empire. So what or who is Melchizedek, and why bring it or him into the conversation at all?

It is fair to be flummoxed by this image of Melchizedek, because he — and yes, Melchizedek is a *he* — makes only one personal appearance in all of the Bible. He pops up briefly, very briefly, during the story of Abraham, early on in the book of Genesis. It so happens that a band of kings went on a raid and, among other things, captured Abraham's nephew Lot. So Abraham went after them with his tribe, defeated them, and freed his nephew. On his return, "King Melchizedek of Salem brought out bread and wine; he was priest of God Most High." This Melchizedek "blessed Abraham.... And Abraham gave him one tenth of everything" (Genesis 14:(8–17), 18–20). And that is it. Except for a verse in Psalm 110 quoted in the Letter to the Hebrews, that is the last we hear of Melchizedek in all the rest of the Old Testament.

So Melchizedek is, at best, a very minor character in the story of Abraham; or maybe not even a character, just a figure whose outline is glimpsed through the fog of primitive history.

So why does the author of the Letter to the Hebrews make so much of this figure? What makes Melchizedek so important to the author's teaching about Jesus? The figure of Melchizedek is important to the Letter's author for two reasons.

First, Melchizedek "was priest of God Most High." Now, so far as the rest of the Old Testament is concerned, the first true "priest of God Most High" was Aaron, the younger brother of Moses; and in the Hebrew religion, nobody could be a priest unless he was descended from Aaron. But here we have a true priest of God Most High long, long before Aaron. Even Abraham, the founding father of Israel, acknowledges as much. For even as Melchizedek brought and offered bread and wine, Abraham gave him a tenth of all the spoils he had captured on his counter-raid. So Melchizedek was the original priest of the Lord God.

Melchizedek was important, secondly, because of his genealogy — or rather, his lack of one. Most males in the Bible are identified by their father's name as well as their own, as in "Simon Peter son of Jonah." Melchizedek has no such identification. He appears "without father, without mother, without genealogy, having neither beginning of days nor end of life," so that "he remains a priest forever" (Hebrews 7:3).

So here you have a mysterious figure named Melchizedek who is a true priest entirely independent of Aaron's lineage, to whom Aaron's forebear Abraham offered tribute, and who has no beginning and no end. And that is just like Jesus — Jesus, as Son of God, has no beginning of days, and as the risen Son of Man he has no end of life. Moreover, he is not only independent of the established priesthood of Aaron, he is also greater than Aaron and all his descendants put together, because he is Son of God. The point that the Letter to the Hebrews is trying to make is this: As Abraham offered tribute to Melchizedek, so should Israel and every other nation offer tribute to Jesus.

But why make Jesus out to be a priest at all? Surely it would be enough to call him Son of God and leave it at that? Not for the Letter to the Hebrews. For the author of that Letter sees Jesus as Son of God precisely in his humanity, in what he did and suffered as a human being. And what he did was offer sacrifice. Only, the sacrifice he offered was not sheep and oxen, as was the case for Aaron's priestly order. The sacrifice that Jesus offered was his very own self, his soul and body. And because he offered such a sacrifice, God took him up into the sanctuary "not made with hands, eternal in the heavens" (2 Corinthians 5:1) — no earthly temple made of stones and decked out with perishable materials, but the very glory of the Father in eternity.

Jesus as priest, as the one who bears our humanity into the very presence of God, becomes the one who intercedes for us in our pains and worries; and because he is the Son of God as well as "a priest forever," God without fail hears his intercession and acts on it.

As once Melchizedek brought forth and offered bread and wine, so now will Jesus take up the bread and wine that we present at the altar, with our prayers and praises, and offer them to the Father. And what does the Father give us back but the very life of his Son, who is both our priest and priest of God Most High.

PASSION

Prophesy to these bones, and say to them: O dry bones, hear the word of the Lord. Thus says the Lord God to these bones: I will cause breath to enter you, and you shall live. I will lay sinews on you, and will cause flesh to come upon you, and cover you with skin, and put breath in you, and you shall live; and you shall know that I am the Lord.

(EZEKIEL 37:4 –6)

If the Spirit of him who raised Jesus from the dead dwells in you, he who raised Christ from the dead will give life to your mortal bodies also through his Spirit that dwells in you.

(ROMANS 8:11)

[Jesus] cried with a loud voice, "Lazarus, come out!" The dead man came out, his hands and feet bound with strips of cloth, and his face wrapped in a cloth. Jesus said to them, "Unbind him, and let him go."

(JOHN 11:43– 44)

This is the Fifth Sunday in Lent. Which means, in effect, the *last* Sunday in Lent; for next Sunday we begin Holy Week, which is a season unto itself; and the Sunday after that is Easter Day. Easter — only two Sundays away! I can hardly believe it. Where has Lent gone? What happened to the time? I had all these plans, all these resolutions — and now, *phhht!* I am not ready for Holy Week to be only seven days away. And why does that feel so unfair?

I suppose the shift in the Church's attitude toward its own practice of Lent has something to do with it. When I came into the Church, Lent was still treated as a grim time, as forty days when one were supposed to hurt — and become a better person for it. And the grimness only got stiffer the deeper we got into Lent. Today, for instance, the Sunday next before Palm Sunday, used to be called Passion Sunday, and it marked a new phase in the Lenten discipline when the Church intensified its penitence. All the crosses and images in the building would be veiled in red cloth; as if it were inappropriate to look on the sign of Christ's triumph in a season devoted to the contemplation of Jesus' sufferings; and the usual doxology at the end of the psalms and canticles was supposed to be omitted, as if it were wrong to ascribe glory to the Father, the Son, and the Holy Spirit.

Under the present dispensation, the theme of the Fifth Sunday in Lent is very different, for all three of today's readings have to do with resurrection. We are taught that resurrection is a theme of joy, not of penitence; a cause for gladness, not for sorrow; a reason for tearing away veils, not for mounting them. Still, the readings, with their witness to the resurrection, may have a certain dissonance in the atmosphere of this liturgy. We may not veil the cross, but this church still wears the purple of penitence, the shades of Lent, and we leave out the *Gloria in excelsis* at the beginning of the eucharist. Do our actions belie the scriptures that the Church appoints for this Sunday? Can we dwell on the sufferings of Christ when today's readings call us to celebrate his victory? Does the contemplation of his passion have anything to do with his resurrection?

The answer may lie in the meaning of the word *passion*. Here we have to be careful. For we modern people tend to think that passion is a good thing, a sign of life and vitality, a mark of joy and energy and commitment. Indeed, what greater condemnation can one modern pass on another, than to say that he or she "lacks passion"? But from ancient days right down to the threshold of our own time, people held a very different view of the matter. Passion was not taken to be a quality that liberated human feeling; passion was regarded as a chronic disability of human nature. It referred to our changeability, to the restlessness of our wills, our lack of stability; our affections are fixed on one object, but then in the twinkling of an eye, we fix them on something else. Passion meant that we were always at the mercy of forces beyond our control, subject to suffering, pain, and death, so that our whole life was spent in passing from one state to another, always losing and never gaining in the process.

But if passion is a failing of our nature, it is also an opportunity — an opportunity for God. The prophet Ezekiel saw a valley full of bones; and these were the remains of a people who had experienced the end of all passion, which was exile and death. But even in their dryness these same bones were still impassioned, still capable of passing over into another state — but this time it was not a state of further dissolution that they experienced, but a new creation under the whispering nurture of God's spirit. And likewise in the gospel: by the word and power of Jesus, one who had been dead and three days in a tomb became impassioned once again — for the passion that Lazarus experienced was his passing from the state of death to the state of renewed life. And that was also the passion of Jesus: He experienced all the impermanence and changeability of our humanity, so that God might change us into the new creation.

So perhaps we can still treat this Fifth Sunday in Lent as Passion Sunday — so long as we realize that passion is no longer just another word for a fleeting existence at the mercy of forces beyond our control and punctuated by pains. For now, today, passion does indeed have something to do with resurrection. Passion is now another word for passover, for that passing-over, that transit into glory. And if we understand that, then resurrection becomes the fulfilment of our passion; it is the revelation of that final change, whereby we shall pass from mortality into the eternal glory of God in Christ.

Holy Week

THE GROUND
OF OBEDIENCE

And being found in human form,
he humbled himself
and became obedient to the point of death
— even death on a cross.

(PHILIPPIANS 2:8)

Then Jesus cried again with a loud voice and breathed his
last.

(MATTHEW 27:50)

St. Paul tells us that Christ "became obedient to the point of death, even death on a cross." That, in a nutshell, is the meaning of the gospel of the passion, the story of how Jesus suffered and died. He endured betrayal, arrest, abandonment, torture, crucifixion, and death — all for the sake of obedience to his Father in heaven.

"Obedience" is a hard word — and in the modern world, even a hateful word. For the present age sets a high premium on the rights (as distinct from the obligations) of the private individual. And this mind-set tends to associate obedience with the quashing of human freedom, with the brutalization of the heart, with the denial of the rights of the individual. The story of the passion seems to offer an example of all this. For the story of the passion could be interpreted as a clash between a lone individual, Jesus, who claimed that he was obeying God, and a pack of authorities, the high priests and the Roman governor, who collaborated in killing him because he would not be obedient to them.

But the story of the passion still turns on Jesus' sense of obligation, not on a sense of his rights as an individual; it was a matter of obedience, not a matter of personal fulfilment — or rather, it was a matter of his being fulfilled only through obedience. And that obedience was still hard, harsh, and brutalizing. The gospel makes it very clear that Jesus did not understand why his Father required him to suffer betrayal, torture, and death on the cross. But still he obeyed. And if we ask why he obeyed, why he still went forward though it appeared that his God and Father had forsaken him, we must go behind obedience and consider its ground. For obedience always takes place in actual situations, when circumstances present us with alternatives; when one of those alternatives is loyalty to a relationship that already exists, faithfulness in a love that has laid claim upon our very existence.

Love was the ground of the obedience of Jesus. He may not have understood why he had to undergo crucifixion, but he followed his love wherever it led, even to the cross. John Donne once said: "Love is a possessory affection." Not that it enables us to possess what we love. On the contrary, "it delivers him that loves into the possession of [what] he loves; it is a

---

1. John Donne, "A Sermon Preached at Pauls Cross ...", 24. Mart. 1616 [1616/17]"; in *The Sermons of John Donne*, eds. George R. Potter and Evelyn M. Simpson, 10 vols. (Berkeley and Los Angeles: University of California Press, 1953–1962), vol. 1, p. 185.

transmutatory affection, it changes him that loves into the very nature of [what] he loves, and he is nothing else."[1]

The love of Jesus was simply the heavenly Father who had sent him, and it was his love for the Father that delivered him into the possession of the Father. Others handed him over to human powers, but he delivered himself to God. That may not be obvious from the story of the passion, a story that ends with Jesus in the possession of the grave and changed into the nature of death. We need to remember what happened on the third day afterwards, to see that, by his obedience, Jesus had indeed commended himself into the hands, into the possession, of the God who is living and true.

Yes, Jesus' love for the Father delivered him into the Father's possession; but it also delivered him into the possession of what God loved. For that is an inevitable consequence of love's possessory nature: to be possessed by what one loves is to be possessed with the very things that the beloved holds dear. And God the Father holds *us* dear. That is why the Father delivered his only Son into the hands, even into the flesh and blood, of human beings. In a sense, God the Father was possessed by humanity, out of love for humanity — possessed in the most personal and intimate way possible, through the Incarnation of his only and eternal Son. And so, for love of the Father, Jesus delivered himself into the hands of sinners; and for the sake of the Father whom he loved above all else, the Son loved the creatures whom the Father held so dear that he would not lose them. Love made the Father send the Son into the world; and love of the Father's will for the world made the Son obey the Father's call to the cross.

The Father's love for the world, and the Son's love for what the Father loves, continue to this very day. In the Holy Eucharist, we pray to the Father, and the Father delivers the Son into our hands, into the hands of each and every one of us — not for the Son's destruction, as on that Friday in Jerusalem so long ago, but for our participation in the Son and the Son's love. This love is still possessory and transforming on God's part; it still delivers Jesus into our possession, it still leads him to submit his eternal glory to the forms of bread and wine, so that he may touch our mortal humanity. But when Jesus touches our humanity through the sacrament, he also reaches out to our love; and that love of ours is no less possessory and no less transforming in nature than his love. The Father gives the body and blood of the Son into our possession, so that we may deliver ourselves into his possession — and be changed into his likeness, "from glory to glory" (2 Corinthians 3:18).

Such is the shape of our obedience to the one whom Jesus taught us to address as "our Father in heaven." It is an obedience whose motive is love, and whose goal is glory. In the meantime, the pains we endure because we are flesh and blood, the frustrations we put up with because we believe in God, the questions our faith makes us launch into the apparent silence of God — all these things are part of the vocation of love, whereby God heals the dimness of our obedience to make us see, and be possessed by, and be changed into Jesus Christ, who, for love of the Father, delivers himself into our possession. Thus possessing, and thus possessed, may we love the One whom Jesus loved — and may we use Holy Week to learn that obedience that loves others because they are beloved by the Father, through the Son, in the power of the Holy Spirit.

The Anointing of Jesus

(John 12:1–11)

"Mary took a pound of costly ointment of pure nard and anointed the feet of Jesus and wiped his feet with her hair; and the house was filled with the fragrance of the ointment." The Lord Jesus understood what this anointing meant: Mary had performed a sacrament of his burial.

Anointing was performed for other, very different reasons too. Aaron, the brother of Moses, was made a priest when a jar of oil was poured over his head — so much oil, that (as Psalm 133 puts it) the ointment ran down upon Aaron's beard and even soaked the collar of his robe. And David was made king over Israel when Samuel poured a cruet of oil over the crown of his head. These anointings were a sacrament, not of entombment, but of enthronement. The pouring of oil upon the head symbolized priestly or kingly power — and more than that, actually conferred the power thus signified.

People go head-first into power; they go feet-first into the grave. Jesus was anointed on his feet, not on his head. So, his anointing at Bethany signified the deprivation of all power, the destruction of all authority, that is death and the grave. The Aaronic priesthood may have endured in Aaron's progeny, but Aaron himself had no more power to bless or sacrifice when his feet were carried over the verge of his tomb. David had his heirs on the throne of Judah, but he himself passed under the sovereign power of death.

And yet, when Mary anointed the feet of Jesus and made a sacrament of his burial, she symbolized more than just his death. The anointing at Bethany signified the great paradox — that Jesus, even in his powerlessness, was to exercise the greatest power of all. One of the prophecies of Christ said that God would put David's enemies under his feet. When Mary anointed the feet of Jesus, she foreshadowed the vanquishment of the last enemy. She did this on Monday, the second day. On Sunday, the eighth day, Jesus, the son of David, will rest his foot on the neck of conquered death.

The Pulley

"And I, when I am lifted up from the earth, will draw all people to myself." So Jesus said to the crowd on the Tuesday of his last week before eternity. St. John the evangelist immediately went on to explain what Jesus meant by these words: "He said this to indicate the kind of death he was to die." And so it came to pass: on Friday Jesus was nailed to a cross as it lay flat on the ground, then the cross was raised to an upright position, so that Jesus was "lifted up from the earth."

But Jesus did more than predict the manner of his death; he also bore witness to the effect of his crucifixion. He said, "I will draw all people to myself." The cross would be like a pole, and he himself would be like a pulley attached to it, by which all others could be raised and exalted, even to that height where his Father in heaven would reach down and grasp his total obedience. For that is the truth about the crucifixion: it was not a loving transaction between Jesus and the world — it was, first and last, a matter of obedience between Jesus and the Father who had sent him.

And yet, precisely because this terrible event was between the Father in glory and the Son on the cross, Jesus would indeed "draw all people to himself." For when he was lifted up on the cross, in obedience to the Father, he pulled taut and straight the ropes that held up the tent of meeting, the shelter in which God and mortals meet face to face. Jesus' obedience on the cross undid the kinks in the cords between heaven and earth, which our slackness had allowed to tangle. And with those kinks now straightened out, there is nothing to stop the tent of meeting from going up around us; and with the tent now sheltering us, we are drawn into the very presence of God.

And then we discover the strangest thing of all: Jesus, whose outstretched hands nailed to the cross were the pulley by which the tent is raised, turns out to be the presence of God in the midst of the tent. He himself is the point at which heaven and earth meet, the one in whom eternal divinity and mortal humanity are united. So his crucified body is where our eyes and our worship should be focused — or at least, where we should be learning to focus. The interior of this tent of meeting as yet appears dim to our sight; we are not used to it, or to the light that inhabits it. But this is what Holy Week is for — and beyond that, what our whole life as Christians is for: that we might learn to focus on the presence of God in the form of his crucified Son. And if we let our beleaguered vision be drawn to him, then in time the whole of our existence will be drawn to him. And more than that: if our lives are drawn to Jesus, the presence of God on the cross, then, by the same reflex that makes others crane their necks upwards where one or two are peering at the heavens, everyone else will be drawn to look at what we are looking at. Thus shall be fulfilled the prophecy Jesus spoke this day, that "he will draw all people to himself" — and into union with his God and Father, in the power of the Holy Spirit.

THE DEPARTURE OF JUDAS

(JOHN 13:30)

"SO, after receiving the piece of bread, [Judas] immediately went out. And it was night." In the gospel according to John, times and seasons always have great importance. Jesus had his last supper with his disciples in the evening; light was still in the sky when this meal began. But by the time Jesus shared the morsel of food with Judas, "it was night." Jesus, the light of the world, was about to begin his dark passage through suffering and death; and the signal for this passage was the departure of Judas Iscariot.

The Evangelist is not interested in why Judas betrayed the Lord. It is enough to know that the departure of the betrayer marked the beginning of the Lord's passion — and that the Lord himself gave his betrayer permission to go. For Jesus said to Judas: "What you are going to do, do quickly." With the departure of Judas, Jesus was free to do what he was going to do: nothing now stood in the way of Jesus to prevent his being lifted up from the earth, or to encumber his drawing all humanity to himself.

At this time of year, our Jewish brothers and sisters prepare for their Passover by scouring their homes and getting rid of all yeast products and every morsel of leavened bread. This is to fulfil the ancient law of the Passover, which ordains that only unleavened bread should be eaten. So with the meal that

Jesus shared with his disciples. In a sense, Judas's departure cleansed the room of the leaven of malice and wickedness, and left only the unleavened bread of the Passover, the true bread of heaven, who is Jesus himself.

And it has come time for us to do the same. All of Lent was supposed to have been a preparation for the three days that begin tomorrow night: it is now time to let go the little treasons in our hearts, to give permission for the sins that betray our love for Jesus to depart from our lives. May God grant us so to cleanse every nook and cranny of our households and communities, that we leave not the slightest morsel of the leaven of malice and wickedness, and may share the unleavened bread of our passover with him who died that we might live, God's only Son, Jesus Christ our Lord.

THE MORSEL

So while reclining next to Jesus, he asked him, "Lord, who is it?"
Jesus answered, "It is the one to whom I give this piece of bread
when I have dipped it in the dish." So when he had dipped the piece
of bread, he gave it to Judas son of Simon Iscariot.

(JOHN 13:25–26)

IT IS the fourth day since Jesus entered Jerusalem, since the crowds of pilgrims met him at the city gates and acclaimed him as "the king who comes in the name of the Lord." And a lot has happened in that short space of time — not so much in the way of events, as in the way people have come to think and feel about Jesus. The acclamations and applause that surrounded him when he rode into the city have died away; crowds no longer run after him wherever he goes, and visitors from foreign lands are no longer trying to cadge an audience with him. The artist-celebrity Andy Warhol once said, "In the future everyone will be world-famous for fifteen minutes." Well, by Wednesday of his week in Jerusalem, it looked as if Jesus' fifteen minutes of being world-famous were already up. The crowds had become bored with him, as they eventually do with every celebrity; only the clutch of disciples who had followed him from Galilee were still around him.

And that is how we find Jesus when the gospel sets us down in the upper room where he is having supper with his disciples. It is of course his last supper; and our imaginations might picture the scene the way Leonardo da Vinci painted it in his canvas, "The Last Supper" — everybody sitting at a long table, as if at a banquet, with Jesus in the chair at the centre. It probably was not like that at all. The give-away is the line in today's gospel that notes that "one of his disciples — the one whom Jesus loved — was *reclining* next to him." Jesus and the disciples ate dinner while reclining on couches — not the kind of couches we have in our living rooms, sofas with backs and arms, but divans, like padded chaises longues. These couches would have been placed on three sides of a low-slung table, and the diners would have lain on their left sides, so that their right hands would be free to take the food from the dishes on the table. It was a cosy arrangement, because Jesus and his disciples would each have had to share a couch with two or more of the others. Jesus, as the host, would have reclined on the couch at the head of the table, with two others. "The disciple whom Jesus loved" reclined on Jesus' left hand, while another disciple reclined on Jesus' right. At ancient Jewish banquets, to be set on the host's right was the position of honour, and it was customary to give this place to an official. The disciples of Jesus had only one official; and that was the one who "kept the common purse," their treasurer. And the treasurer was Judas Iscariot.

So there was Jesus, reclining at supper on a couch with "the beloved disciple" on his left and Judas Iscariot on his right, in the place of honour. And then Jesus hears a squeak in the cosmos, a muffled "uh-oh" in a remote corner of creation, and he knows that it is time for a decision to be made. It is not a decision that he himself has to make, for he has already taken it. No, it is the moment of decision for somebody else, the moment when that person has to decide whether he is for or against the Lord. So Jesus announces, "Very truly, I tell you, one of you will betray me." The disciples are startled, and they look at one another, thoroughly abashed. Whom could he be talking about? Which one of them would do such a thing?

From his seat farther down the table, Peter caught the eye of the beloved disciple, raised his eyebrows, and nodded toward Jesus. The beloved disciple leaned back and, whispering, asked the Lord who it was. Jesus murmured back, "It is the one to whom I give this piece of bread when I have dipped it in the dish." In the ancient world, dipping bread or some other piece of food in the sauce and handing to the person beside you was a high compliment; it was a sign of special favour for that person, a mark that you held his friendship so dear to you that you would rather smear your own fingers with the sauce than see him do so. By making this gesture, Jesus would not only be identifying the traitor. He would also be performing what he and his culture regarded as a supreme act of hospitality and friendship — and thus making one last appeal to the traitor's better nature, that he renounce his intended course and remain Jesus' honoured friend as well as a favoured disciple. Then came the moment: "when Jesus had dipped the piece of bread, he gave it to Judas son of Simon Iscariot," to the treasurer, the disciple in the position of honour on Jesus' right.

And Judas accepted the bread from Jesus' hand. He may not have known that Jesus thereby identified him as the betrayer, but he certainly would have understood the moral and social consequences of his accepting the morsel that Jesus offered him. In the ancient world, the worst possible sin was to violate someone's hospitality, to do harm to someone with whom you had broken bread, had shared a meal. Judas accepted the morsel from Jesus' hand, but did not renounce his intention to betray Jesus. Now he was not only a traitor to the cause; he had put himself beyond the pale of human society. The gospel puts

Judas's situation in the harshest light: "After he received the piece of bread, Satan entered into him. Jesus said to him, 'Do quickly what you are going to do.' ... So, after receiving the piece of bread, Judas immediately went out. And it was night."

That evening has come again. We are members of a society that, like the crowds in Jerusalem during that April week two thousand years ago, may still be curious about Jesus, but is no longer committed to him. We alone are left, to share a meal with him. For that is what the eucharist, the celebration of the Lord's Supper, is about. It is about sharing a meal with Jesus; I or some other priest might be presiding at the table, but Jesus is really our host. And though we stand or kneel at the tables of our eucharist, instead of reclining on couches around it, yet each and every one of us is at his right hand, in the position of honour. And he offers each and every one of us a piece of bread, a morsel of his own life, saying as he enters into our lives, "Do quickly what you are going to do."

And what shall that be? Will we be true to his hospitality and friendship, and do his will, loving him and the Father and the Holy Spirit with all our heart, and all our soul, and all our mind, and all our strength, and love our neighbours as ourselves? Or will we practise little treasons, garden-variety betrayals, of his love for us? When we go out after receiving him, the true bread of life, will it be night, though the sun shines; or will it be daylight, the daylight of those who walk with Jesus, the light of the world?

The Paschal Triduum

THE TWOFOLD COMMANDMENT

This is my commandment, that you love one another as I have loved you.

(JOHN 15:12)

Do this in remembrance of me.

(1 CORINTHIANS 11:24)

WE call this day Maundy Thursday. The name comes from the Latin word *mandatum*, which the English of the Middle Ages turned into the word "maundy." It simply means "command" or "commandment." So the "maundy" of Maundy Thursday refers to the com*maund*ment that, according to John's gospel, our Lord gave to his disciples when he said: "This is my commandment, that you love one another even as I have loved you."

But the other gospels, and St. Paul in his first Letter to the Corinthians, tell us of another commandment, a second "maundy," which Jesus gave his disciples on this very same day. For it was in the evening of this day that our Lord instituted the eucharist, the mystery of the new passover, and commanded: "Do this in remembrance of me." So, we have two "maundies," two commandments, to observe today — or rather, one commandment in a twofold aspect. For the commandment of love and the institution of the eucharist are inseparable: they are one "maundy."

First, there is the commandment that we love one another even as Christ has loved us. It is always difficult to speak about love, never more so than from the pulpit; and the preacher does well to remember the words of Eliza Doolittle in the musical *My Fair Lady*: "Don't talk of love, show me!" So, how can I show you?

Let us consider the setting of the commandment, the great "maundy" of love. Jesus was at supper with his disciples, and the supper was somehow connected with the Jewish Passover. The first lesson tonight, a reading from the book of Exodus, reminds us what that was all about: it was a feast, a banquet, in memorial of Israel's liberation from slavery in Egypt. More than that, God set his people free, so that they might go forth and take possession of the land that God had promised to them. The whole point of the passover, then, was possession. Israel's liberation was complete only when the people had occupied, and were actually enjoying, "the land flowing with milk and honey." So it is with love. Love too is a liberation, a liberation of the heart, a liberation that is only complete when the heart possesses and actually enjoys its beloved. But this same liberation can become complete only if we go forth from ourselves — only if we pass over from ourselves to our beloved. This does not mean that we lose our selves or become absorbed by our beloved. By their passover from Egypt to the promised land the people of Israel did not cease to be what and who they were. No more do we cease to be ourselves by this passover of love. On the contrary, like Israel, we become what we were always meant to be: we come to inhabit and possess and enjoy our own truth.

And yet to love, truly to love, does indeed mean that we

inhabit and enjoy our own truth only so far as we enable our beloved to be, not what we are, but themselves. Israel did not enjoy the promised goods of the land of Canaan until the people tilled the land and made it fruitful: and it was only by making the land fruitful that they became fruitful. So with love: we do not possess and enjoy our beloved, unless we make them fruitful in themselves, unless we nurture and tend whatever befits their own truth and happiness. And so Jesus commanded us to love one another. Christian people have their truth, possess their individual integrity, only by practising mutual passovers, each passing over to the other, to make each other fruitful in all good works.

So then, the love that Jesus commands is a paschal, a passover love; and perhaps this suggests to you the eucharistic connection. For the Holy Eucharist is the new passover-feast, the memorial of that sovereign Love who passed from the house of suffering and death over into the promised land of resurrection. By sharing this memorial of Christ's passover, we ourselves join in that passover and go our way to enter and take possession of the same land of promise. As Paul told the Corinthians: "As often as you eat this bread, and drink the cup, you proclaim the Lord's death until he comes."

Now, consider what we do when we eat and drink. We take something in, we consume it and possess it in the completest possible manner; we may even enjoy it, unless it be broccoli or lima beans. But whatever it is, when we eat or drink something, we make it our own: we change it into the sort of energy our bodies can use; we may even be said to change the food into our body. So it is with the bread and the wine of the eucharist, the outward and visible sacrament first on the altar and then in our mouths: we eat and drink the visible signs, and they become our possessions.

But we have Christ's own word, and the assurance of the Holy Spirit, that when we eat this bread, we receive the true Bread that comes down from above, who is Jesus Christ, and when we drink this cup, we share the vintage of the true Vine, who is the same Jesus Christ. In this feast, which is the banquet of his new passover, Jesus Christ really does give himself into our possession. He sticks to our ribs as surely as any nourishment can do; he becomes flesh of our flesh, and one with us, as any other kind of true sustenance will do. When he commanded his disciples to love one another, our Lord added, "even as I have loved you." In this banquet, he himself practises the passover-love that he commands: he passes over to those whom he loves; he passes over to us, that he might establish us and make us fruitful, yes, that he might have in us his own integrity and truth.

And yet, by this eucharistic passover, Jesus is not consumed, he is not absorbed by us. He remains still and ever the same, still and ever whole. The Lord who gives himself to us here is not a corpse, a dead thing: the Lord we here receive is the crucified Lord who has risen again, the same Lord whom no door could shut out, whom no room could contain, whom no human vision could simply comprehend. The Lord Jesus passes over to our possession in the eating of this bread and the drinking of this cup, so that we might pass over to his risen life — so that we might become *his* possession, *his* delight, and *his* joy. And so, Christ's presence in this sacrament is not an end itself: Christ ordains his presence here for the sake of our passover to the presence of his Father in heaven. For the union of the Son with the Father in the Holy Spirit — the very life of the Trinity whom we adore — this is our own promised land, the land for which we are liberated that we might enter in and possess it; the life of God the most holy Trinity is the fullness of our love, the integrity and truth of our being.

This is the love with which Christ has loved us, the passover-love that draws us forth toward his unity with the Father and the Spirit. And if this is his love for us, this also is the love that he commands us to have for one another. It is a love that practises the mutual passover, where each of us seeks in the other the Christ who dwells in us that we might dwell in him; where each of us passes over to the other, no longer with that jealousy that desires only possession and consumption, but with that affection that seeks to nurture the other and to make them fruitful in all good works — fruitful in the greatest good of all, which is the love of Christ Jesus, the Paschal Lamb, the Bread from heaven, the true Vine, our meat and drink, our Lord and, with the Father and the Holy Spirit, our promised land.

THE SHELTER
OF GOD'S WINGS

*Jesus answered [Pilate], "You would have no power over me
unless it had been given you from above."*

(JOHN 19:11)

*For you have been my help,
and in the shadow of your wings I sing for joy.*

(PSALM 63:7)

The story that we tell on Good Friday is a story of denial,
degradation, and death; a story in which one person, Jesus of Nazareth, suffers betrayal by Judas, denial by Peter,
persecution by the high priests, condemnation at the hands of
Pilate, brutality at the hands of the Roman soldiers, and death
due to shock and suffocation while nailed to a cross. There was
still one more horror, a horror that caused and consummated
all these other horrors. At one point in his passion Jesus told
Pilate: "You would have no power over me unless it had been
given you from above." In other words, Jesus suffered because
God ordained it. He was certainly the victim of human sin, of
the power that makes us cowardly and fearful, violent and abusive; but it also appears that, even before human sin laid hands
on him, Jesus was the victim of his own Father's will. And therein
lies the elemental horror of Good Friday.

Why would God call for Jesus to be a victim? And why would the almighty Father demand such a degrading sacrifice from the incarnate Son? The Church has always tried to answer this scandalous question by talking about the love of God, God's love for us and all the human race. But again — what kind of love is it that sends one's own child to death in order to embrace others? From this perspective, talking about God's love only deepens the horror of the passion and reveals the scandal of the cross at its starkest. We need to begin elsewhere, and to search out the difference between ourselves and God before we can start to talk about the love of God at work in the murder of Jesus.

⁓

When I was young, my parents owned a farm in New England. Most of our property was studded with stands of spruce and tamarack, or simply overgrown. But across the street from our house lay an open field, and there, every summer, I would be sent to break the ground and plant various crops, then to water and pull up weeds. In the months of June and July, the sun blistered my skin and taught me the meaning of the primordial curse, "By the sweat of your face you shall eat bread until you return to the ground" (Genesis 4:19A). The only relief in all that sun-seared field was a single maple tree, huge and luxuriant in its leafage; and there, in the green shadow of that lone maple, I would take my breaks, to wipe the sweat off my face and to blink the sun's glare out of my eyes. I used to curse the sun just for shining, but I blessed the tree for providing such shelter. As the psalmist said of the Lord, so I said of that tree, "Under the shadow of your wings I will rejoice."

Of course it was silly of me to curse the sun for shining; it was not the sun's fault that I sweated, or that I would sleep fitfully at night because I had let myself get so sunburned during the day. The sun was just being the sun, and I had failed to respect its power.

Perhaps God, the sheer holiness of God, is something like that. We cannot bear contact with God, any more than we can bear too much contact with the rays of the sun. It is not because God is angry with us, or set on vengeance; it is just because God is God, and we are mortal beings, creatures of flesh and blood. The prophet Isaiah once heard the Lord God say: "My thoughts are not your thoughts, nor are your ways my ways. For as the heavens are higher than the earth, so are my ways higher than your ways, and my thoughts than your thoughts (Isaiah 55:8–9)." There is a difference, an infinite difference, between ourselves and God; and the difference is dangerous to beings of flesh and blood.

We humans have always struggled with this difference between ourselves and God, as we try to understand it and still believe that, because God created us, God loves us. One of the ways in which we try to make the difference easier to handle is by focusing on our own sins. Make no doubt about it, the sins are really there, and we must never pretend that they are not. We have indeed violated the holiness of God by the things we have done and by the things we have failed to do, by our malice and our greed, by our violence and our selfishness, by our laziness and our lovelessness. But our sins are a function of the difference between ourselves and God — they are not the cause or explanation of that difference, but one of the ways in which we respond to it; and our difference from God remains even after God's own mercy has forgiven our sins. For we still remain creatures, not gods, and God still remains God, uncreated, unbounded by space and time, unafflicted by the gap between thought and action, feeling and understanding.

Throughout the Bible runs the conviction that we humans cannot see God and survive the encounter; the power of God, the very reality of God, is too much for us to bear. This conviction informs the New Testament as well as the Old Testament; but in the New Testament, this same conviction is balanced, even overborne by another conviction — that God sent his only Son, Jesus Christ, to make us capable of bearing the reality of God. "The same God who said, 'Let light shine out of darkness,' has shone in our hearts to give the light of the knowledge of the glory of God in the face of Jesus Christ" (2 Corinthians 4:6). Seeing the face of Jesus, we see God — and survive the encounter.

But the face that we see is the face of one who was crowned with thorns and nailed to a cross. Jesus died bearing our sins, that is true; but he also died bearing what we humans, as created beings, could not endure, the full brunt of the unmitigated holiness of God. Jesus on the cross was like that maple tree in the field where I worked as a teenager; he stretched out his limbs to shelter us from the searing impact of God's reality upon our exposed humanity. Or to quote the psalm again, "In the shadow of your wings I sing for joy." The wings of God are the arms of Jesus nailed to the cross.

⌒ ⌒

Perhaps now we can begin to talk about the love of God, and start to deal with our original question, why the loving Father would will the crucifixion of his incarnate Son. For it is indeed God's own love that stretched out the protecting limbs of the crucified, to provide us with shelter from the burning heat that sears the vast field of creation. Having created us, God desires us to enjoy the divine glory, to dwell with health and even pleasure in the light of the Almighty, to be glad in the presence of the three-personed Holy One. But God also knows that the divine reality is too much for us to bear. So what did God do? The Father sent the only Son, first to share our nature and condition, and then to stretch out his arms on the cross "for us and for our salvation." The Church confesses that Jesus was both truly God and truly human. As a human he willingly accepted death on the cross to absorb all the raw power of divinity that we cannot bear; as God, he converted that searing, sun-like power into shade for us, so that we might dwell in peace and know the Almighty no longer by his difference from us but by his nearness to us, by the cool shade of the cross and by the spangling of the leaves above us, as the Spirit breathes through the limbs of the one tree of life.

Thus, the crucified is the only way we can know God and live, for the crucified is God — God in the tree that shelters us from the power we could not otherwise bear. So, let us remember what the only Son of God suffered for us; and even as we know that this Friday was once a day of death on a cross, let us also remember that this Friday is good; for on this day, the day of Jesus' passion and death, we are also called to rejoice under the shadow of his wings.

April Fool's

We call Good Friday good, even though it is the day we keep the anniversary of a death — the death of the Son of God. There does not seem to be much good about this Friday; and we may wonder why we call it *Good* Friday. The answer has to do with the person whose death we remember today. On this day two thousand years ago, Jesus hung from the cross, and the Son of God bled to death on that tree. Our Anglo-Saxon ancestors, long, long ago in the early Middle Ages, followed the logic of such a truth and called this day God Friday. Now, God and good are closely related words, not only in sound but also in meaning; for God is good. And so, as time passed, God Friday became broader in sound, until our nearer ancestors got used to saying Good Friday. They looked upon the cross on which God, the Son of God, was hanged to death, and they confessed that it was an act of God's goodness to us. For Jesus died for us and for our salvation; and so far as human beings are concerned, could there be any better good than that? So this is Good Friday, because it is the Friday when God was so good as to die for us.

I recall a year when Good Friday fell on the first of April, a day that has another name, and another sort of behaviour, associated with it. We call it April Fool's Day; and it is a day when, if we are not exactly bad, neither are we exactly good. It is a day for being silly, not solemn; it is a day when we try to play tricks on our family and friends and, in a light-hearted way, without malice, try to make fools of them.

Good Friday and April Fool's Day — what a conjunction! Indeed, we might think it a contradiction in terms. For solemnity and silliness do not seem to go together; Good Friday seems to demand that we suspend our sense of humour, while April Fool's Day seems to suspend the rules that force us to be serious. And I suppose we all know what we ought to do: on Good Friday we ought to be good, good and serious, because this is *God's* day; and God, we know, does not have a sense of humour.

But *do* we know that God has no sense of humour? Can we be so sure that God is always solemn and serious? Perhaps Good Friday, God Friday, is also God's April Fool's Day — even when it does not fall on the first of April.

And on whom would God play tricks? Whom would the Almighty try to make a fool of? Not us, I think; since God is good, God gave us a sense of humour, which is one of our best defences against the fear of death. And come to think of it, there is nothing so solemn, so relentlessly serious, as death. Death never laughs, never cracks so much as a smile; death always stands on its honour, and does not know how to play or have fun. God had fun when he created the universe and all the vast array of worlds, with all their different creatures. There was chuckling in heaven while the Almighty fashioned this earth, and laughter when the Most High spread out the heavens. Death can't stand it; can't stand the merriment and playfulness of God, and so it continually tries to shush it up, like a raw substitute teacher who has lost control of his or her class. But the only way death knows how to silence God's laughter is by trying to swallow us and everything else God has made. Death is indeed the original kill-joy, because death seeks literally to kill what God delights in and gives God joy, which is us creatures.

But God is God, and will not be stifled. So think of this day, think of what happened on this day outside the walls of Jerusalem, as if it were God's April Fool's Day. God the Son gave himself to death, and to the forces of death, in order to make a fool of death. For our common enemy, stiff and deadly serious, thought it had swallowed one more servant of God and put down the riot that this man, this Jesus of Nazareth had threatened to raise in the class of life. And there was indeed silence on Golgotha, on the place of a skull where Jesus was crucified, when he finally breathed his last. But there too was the joke. For death had not swallowed just another creature; death had swallowed God. The result was a truly cosmic case of heartburn, a massive pain in the gut of death; and on the third day, death was forced to gorge out the life it had swallowed on Good Friday — and with that life, the lives of all those who had served God faithfully in their generation, before the Son of God came in our flesh.

It was a trick played not on us but on death; on Good Friday, God Friday, God made an April Fool of death. And since the Almighty chuckled in glory, perhaps we may allow ourselves to smile.

OUT OF THE ORDINARY

Every Good Friday we join in telling the long, very dramatic story of the passion of our Lord. And being only human, we may think that, because the telling of this story preoccupied us, so the events it recounted must have preoccupied Jerusalem and indeed, the whole world at the time they actually happened. After all, this was the trial and execution of the Son of God; and we assume that everybody at the time must have been just as interested, or at least just as caught up, in the crucifixion of Jesus as we are today.

But we would be mistaken. The people in Jerusalem that day busied themselves with their ordinary business. True, those who were Jewish also had to prepare for the Passover, their great religious festival, which began that night; but that was only one thing more on top of all the ordinary things they had to do every other day of the year. If they were Roman legionaries or Greek merchants, it was a day like any other, except that the festival had brought larger crowds into Jerusalem and posed a few more headaches for policing the city. But Pilate the governor hardly spent a lot of time on the case of the rabbi from Galilee, and he certainly did not need to commit all the troops at his disposal to the execution of that rabbi. He simply told one of his subordinates to take care of the matter, and that subordinate assigned a small detail of soldiers to carry out what would have been a fairly routine duty for them, all in a day's work for troops policing a small part of a large empire.

And what of our own day? You and I, of course, are here because we have an inkling, or perhaps more than an inkling, that this day is important; important not just for us but for all human beings. And for the time being, the powers that be, society at large, indulge us. They have made this a statutory holiday, a day off, so that people like us may come to church and worship our God for dying not only on our behalf but also on behalf of the whole world. And yet the vast majority of people in our society are quite content to go about their ordinary business on this day; they may not have to go to work, but they can spend the day doing the ordinary sorts of things they do on Saturdays or Sundays, without a thought for the God who was nailed to a cross. So the affairs of the world do not seem to have changed very much; and just as the people of Jerusalem, Jews and Romans alike, went about their ordinary lives on the day that Jesus died, so most of the people in this province, in this country, and on this continent carry on with their ordinary lives on this Good Friday.

It is ordinary to be damned. For damnation is to live without God, to have so little sense of God's presence as to think that one can afford a life without Jesus; and it is a common, everyday, garden-variety sort of thing to have no time for God our creator and the Son of God our redeemer. And we ourselves must be careful not to congratulate ourselves too readily for being here today. Jesus did not die so that our society could have one day off a week, and a few other days-off in the year too. Nor did he die so that those of us who *do* remember him, and *do* worship him on those days, need remember and worship him only on those days, and sink the remembrance and worship of him on all other days. Religion is all fine and good on Sundays, and maybe Good Friday as well; but we think we must get on with life, and go about our ordinary business.

But again I say, it is ordinary to be damned; it is an extraordinary thing, a thing amazingly out of the ordinary, to be saved. And that is why Jesus died on this day — to release us, and all the world, from the ordinary, from the bonds and bounds that lock us into the pains of our humanity. It is for freedom that Christ has set us free — the freedom of knowing, of loving, of enjoying the life of God, who made us and longs to embrace us with glory. God is not honoured or truly worshipped, if Jesus his Son is remembered only once a week and on spare special occasions like Good Friday. God is truly worshipped, and the reason for Good Friday is genuinely honoured, only if we set about freeing our hearts from the quotidian courses, the routine bounds and bonds that enclose and shackle our lives, and allow the cross of Jesus to carry us out of the ordinary into the transcendent freedom of God, our maker, our redeemer, and our lover.

EARTHQUAKES AND ANGELS

*After the sabbath, as the first day of the week was dawning,
Mary Magdalene and the other Mary went to see the tomb.
And suddenly there was a great earthquake; for an angel of
the Lord, descending from heaven, came and rolled back the
stone and sat on it. His appearance was like lightning, and
his clothing white as snow.*

(MATTHEW 28:1–3)

We all know people who cannot tell a joke to save their lives. They could have faultless material, a story that for any other comedian would guarantee laughs at every turn; but in the hands of these sorry souls, the same material, the same story falls flat. They may get a few giggles here and there, but for the most part the audience responds with blank incomprehension or downright embarrassment. I sympathize with such people, because I am one of them; a joke or funny story, when I tell it, might as well be a report from Statistics Canada, for all the laughter it gets. I think my problem is, that I lack what is called timing. I muddle the story with details, which I invariably get wrong, and then I try to gild the lily with more details than are necessary. So, by the time I reach the punch line, it has all the punch of a thin mist.

The same thing can happen when it comes to much more serious matters, in the telling of stories that are anything but jokes or funny anecdotes. It happens, for example, in Matthew's account of the resurrection of Jesus. You would think that the resurrection of Jesus would be astounding enough in itself, not to need any more miracles and wonders. But Matthew does just that: he gilds the Easter lily with extra wonders. Alone of all the evangelists, Matthew tells of an earthquake on earth and an angel descending from heaven to roll back the stone at the door of the tomb and then sit on it. It is as if Matthew wants to improve upon the basic miracle, the fact that Jesus was raised from the dead. But his telling has become so top-heavy with incredible details, that when he gets to the encounter Mary Magdalene and "the other Mary" had with the risen Lord himself, it ends up feeling like an anti-climax.

But I am being much too hard on St. Matthew. Like the other three evangelists — indeed, like all Christian believers — he is trying to talk about the impossible. For nothing in the world, nothing in the shape of things as we know them, has anything to compare with the resurrection of Jesus. We have all heard about people who were clinically dead coming back to life, either on an operating table in hospital or (horrifically) in tombs after they were buried. But that is not resurrection. Resurrection means something completely different from the resuscitation of a corpse. It means an event that does not fit into time and space, into the way things normally work in the world.

Resurrection does not fit into the categories we take for granted, because it changes them. When he was raised, Jesus still had some sort of body, for Mary Magdalene and the other Mary were able to take hold of his feet — and one cannot grab the feet of a ghost, much less touch and hug a figment of one's imagination. But by the same token there was something immeasurably strange about the risen Jesus; and it is this strangeness that frustrates every attempt to describe the Lord as he was on the third day. It is much easier to talk about earth-quakes and angels than to say what Jesus was like after his resurrection. And so, talking about earthquakes and angels becomes a way of suggesting something unheard of, a way of hinting at an unspeakable change in the shape of the universe.

And we continue to struggle with that unspeakable change. Because Jesus was raised from the dead, never to die again, the universe is the same, only very, very different — and the difference is what eludes us, caught as we are in the dimensions of time and space. What separates us believers from the rest of the world, is that we have received just enough grace to be patient with what eludes our grasp — just enough grace to be patient with God, who created the universe out of nothing and brought Jesus out of death. It is only when our patience fails us for a moment, that we start looking for earthquakes and angels; it is only when we lose a little of our nerve, that we start to gild the Easter lily with extra signs and wonders. Then we miss the point of the joke that God played upon death, and miss the laughter in heaven as Jesus steps back into the world from the tomb. Believing in the resurrection is a matter of living with an unspeakable change in the universe — and chuckling along with God.

TERROR AND AMAZEMENT

So they went out and fled from the tomb, for terror and amazement had seized them; and they said nothing to anyone, for they were afraid.

(MARK 16:8)

Easter is supposed to be a time of joy and exultation, and the good news of Christ's resurrection is supposed to make us shout "Alleluia!" And indeed, for much of the Great Vigil of Easter, we do just that: we seem to say, sing, call out "Alleluia!" at almost every turn. Moreover, the theme of joy, sometimes calm, sometimes strident, runs through the readings we hear and the hymns we sing. Until just now, until St. Mark's account of the resurrection itself. It is, of all things, the very gospel that has rained on our Easter parade.

For St. Mark does not give us a scene full of joy and exultation. On the contrary, as Mark tells the story, the risen Lord does not even make an appearance. All we get is an empty tomb, "a young man, dressed in a white robe," and three women — women who "fled from the tomb, for terror and amazement had seized them; and they said nothing to anyone, for they were afraid." And that is how Mark's gospel ends — not on a note of triumphant joy but on a note of alarm, terror, and flight. There are no alleluias in Mark's account of the resurrection, only the sound of three pairs of feet scurrying away — and then silence.

But why should the resurrection have come as such a shock? After all, the Scriptures had foretold it, as we heard in the reading from the book of the prophet Ezekiel. And, if the gospels are to be trusted, Jesus himself foretold that he would be raised again on the third day. So it is not as if Mary, the other Mary, Salome, and the rest of our Lord's disciples had no warning of the event. And yet when Easter actually happened, when Jesus was indeed raised from the dead, the first three disciples to hear the news went into shock and fled the scene as fast as their fright could carry them.

Perhaps Mary Magdalene, the other Mary, and Salome were right to be afraid, right to be scared out of their wits. For the resurrection of Jesus does not belong to the world as we know it. Sweating and quaking with fear, betrayal by friends, the injustice of rulers, and a lingering death — all the things that Jesus endured on Good Friday, are things that belong to the world as we know it. Perhaps that is why Christians, down through the ages, have found it easier to remember Good Friday than to celebrate Easter. For, much as we dread it, death is part of the way things are, and there have been those of us who dealt with it on just that basis — if not as a friend, then at least as a stranger whose arrival comes as no surprise. But resurrection is not part of the way things are, and there is no way to prepare for it. When Jesus was raised from the dead, it came as a shock to the whole system of time and space — an even greater shock to the system, to "the way things are," than death.

And that is because the resurrection marks the moment when the system, "the ways things are," is hit with the raw glory of God. To be sure, God is goodness, light, grace, and love. But above all else, God is glory — and the glory of God is nothing ordinary. God created all things, but God is not a part of the way things are. God made time and space, the dimensions in which we live and die; but when God the Father raised his Son from the dead, he did not merely bend the rules of time and space — he broke them and made them new.

We have a saying: "Better the devil you know than the devil you don't know." And that saying goes double for reality. Better the world as we know it, even if it includes death, than the resurrection we don't know. Mary Magdalene, the other Mary, and Salome fled from the God they had known yet not known. The God they had known was the God who had promised a resurrection, an indefinite possibility; the God they had not yet known was the God who fulfilled his own promise and made the resurrection, the definite fact of his Son raised from the dead; and this is the God they fled.

But tonight we make up for their moment of panic; we have come after them, and we stand from whence they fled. We stand, though we too may be confused, or perplexed, or even afraid at the news that Jesus of Nazareth, God's only Son, has risen from the dead — at the news that God is even greater and more glorious than we imagined, even truer and more faithful to his own promise than we understood. Yet the strength not to flee, the courage to stand and believe, is also part of the promise of this God. It is by God's gift that we have come to this moment, and it is by God's own love for us that we are able to feel the first tremors of something strange — joy that the world was not entirely as we thought, and gladness that, yes, Christ the Lord is indeed risen this night.

THE RESURRECTION
AND MARY MAGDALENE

*[Mary Magdalene] turned around and saw Jesus standing
there, but she did not know that it was Jesus. Jesus said to
her, "Woman, why are you weeping? Whom are you looking
for?" Supposing him to be the gardener, she said to him, "Sir,
if you have carried him away, tell me where you have laid
him, and I will take him away." Jesus said to her, "Mary!"
She turned and said to him in Hebrew, "Rabbouni!" (which
means Teacher). Jesus said to her, "Do not hold on to me,
because I have not yet ascended to the Father."*

(JOHN 20:14–17A)

Mary Magdalene was weeping outside the empty
tomb of the crucified Jesus, when she turned and saw
someone standing close by. She thought it was the gardener.
Then the person spoke her name, and she recognized who it
was. It was Jesus, and she responded: "Rabbouni!" — "Dearest
Master!"

In this episode faith has two things to meditate. First, Mary
failed to recognize Jesus the minute she saw him; and second,
she recognized him only when he spoke her name.

In the first place, Mary did not know that the person standing there was Jesus; she thought he was the gardener. This was
the same Jesus who suffered, died, and was buried, but some

change had happened to him: he was the same, only different. What that difference might have been, is suggested by the word "resurrection." But it is only suggested, for the meaning of resurrection always seems to be just beyond our grasp.

Jesus told Mary, "Do not try to cling to me, for I have not yet ascended to the Father." Jesus is alive, yes — but alive with a being no longer simply human and created. Jesus, the Resurrection and the Life, is alive with the life of the glory of his Father in heaven — with a life that cannot be contained, or defined, or explained by the categories natural to flesh and blood, in the dimensions of space and time. Natural existence is closed off, and finally sealed in, by the door of death; but Jesus has burst that barrier, and his humanity is now entirely open to God. What a tremendous change! — a change that turns natural existence inside-out, that pulls the rug from under the present world order and sends it sprawling. So it is no wonder that Mary Magdalene did not instantly recognize Jesus, the One who is himself the Resurrection and the Life.

And this initial failure of recognition was in no way Mary's fault. Indeed, she could never have recognized Jesus unless the Risen One had called her by name. Jesus first had to acknowledge Mary as his disciple before she could recognize him and know the joy of this recognition. This fits in with a word spoken earlier on in John's gospel, where the Jesus of this gospel says that the Good Shepherd "calls his own sheep by name and leads them out ... for they know his voice" (John 10:3–4). It was not the face or figure of the risen Jesus that Mary recognized. It was his voice that she knew; and it was this voice addressing her, and calling her by her own name, that gave her power to recognize the Speaker in his risen glory.

The knowledge of Jesus, the knowledge of the Resurrection

and the Life, is always a gift that only Jesus himself can give; and it is a gift that he gives only to those who truly belong to his own flock — to those whom he acknowledges and draws to himself. Not everyone is so called, not everyone is made capable of hearing and recognizing the shepherd-voice of the resurrection. That capability, that power of hearing, like the resurrection itself, comes from above and belongs to the order of divine life, where Jesus now dwells with his Father in union with the Spirit of holiness.

As then, so now. Then, Jesus eluded Mary's recognition in the garden until he called her by name; now, he comes to us in the forms of bread and wine, and might elude our recognition, unless he called us, each one of us, by name. But so he does; and we have power, by the grace of his voice, to know and celebrate his presence in our eucharists. His voice is as truly present in our celebrations as his body and blood, his life; and if our hearing of this voice is faithful to him, each of us shall be in the space of Mary Magdalene. The voice of Jesus will call us each by name, and each of us will turn our lives around to meet him and exclaim in recognition of the one who is here for us, "Rabbouni! — Dearest Master!"

8 - use of meditation/etc. → apologia for
         piscatorial theologica;

23-25 - Temptation - us & JC → 24/para 3

56 - 10 Commandments = can't keep faith with God
         unless we keep faith with our neighbours

60 - rationalizes a building project

62 - "God" = what not who Almighty is

x95 - "But the story of the passion turns..."

165 - funeral sermon

- repetition - "show me" 161/ seeing is
                                        believing 146/

- application - posterity & church/sacramental circle
         - e.g., 134/ 187/ 194/

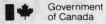Government
of Canada

Gouvernement
du Canada

ACTION REQUEST
FICHE DE SERVICE

To — A	File No. — Dossier N°
	Date

From — De

☐ Please call / Prière d'appeler	Tel. No. — N° de tél.	Ext. — Poste

| ☐ Returned your call / Vous a rappelé | ☐ Will call again / Vous rappellera | ☐ Wants to see you / Désire vous voir |

| Date | Time — Heure | Message received by / Message reçu par |

☐ Action / Donner suite	☐ Approval / Approbation	☐ Note & return / Noter et retourner
☐ Comments / Commentaires	☐ Draft reply / Projet de réponse	☐ Note & forward / Noter et faire suivre
☐ As requested / Comme demandé	☐ Signature	☐ Note & file / Noter et classer

GC 12E

7540-21-868-3907

THE EMPTY TOMB

Then Peter and the other disciple set out and went toward the tomb. The two were running together, but the other disciple outran Peter and reached the tomb first. He bent down to look in and saw the linen wrappings lying there, but he did not go in. Then Simon Peter came, following him, and went into the tomb. He saw the linen wrappings lying there, and the cloth that had been on Jesus' head, not lying with the linen wrappings but rolled up in a place by itself. Then the other disciple, who reached the tomb first, also went in, and he saw and believed; for as yet they did not understand the scripture, that he must rise from the dead. Then the disciples returned to their homes.

(JOHN 20:3–10)

Some people have trouble taking a statement at face value; their minds go whirr and click-click-click as they figure out whether there is any exception to be made. You all have met at least one person like that; he stands before you right now. I've been this way since I was nine or ten, when I discovered the meaning of the magic phrase, "Not necessarily." And with that phrase I drove my mother bananas for the next seven years. Mother would say, "Right is right and wrong is wrong." And I would say, "Not necessarily." Mother would say, "The rain in Spain falls mainly on the plain." And I would say, "Not necessarily." Mother would say, "Cut that out, Stephen; you know how your saying that irritates me." And I would say, "Not necessarily." And so it would go. Happily I went off to university before she killed me; and even if she had done, she would not necessarily have been convicted by any jury in the country.

Here it is, Easter Day; and the gospel for today is the story of the discovery by Mary Magdalene and two other disciples that the tomb where Jesus had been buried, was empty. This one fact, the empty tomb, used to be given enormous importance in Christian talk about the resurrection. Human testimony can be fallible, and humans can make mistakes; so it was best to test every human word by the physical evidence. Mary Magdalene might be wrong about what she really saw and heard; Simon Peter and the other disciple might be wrong as well; so might all the other disciples who claimed to have seen the risen Lord Jesus. But you cannot argue with the empty tomb. Jesus was not in the tomb; therefore he must have been raised from the dead. In other words, the empty tomb proves the resurrection. Right?

Not necessarily....

Just consider the story told in today's gospel. "Early on the first day of the week, while it was still dark, Mary Magdalene came to the tomb" where Jesus had been laid after his crucifixion and death, "and [she] saw that the stone had been removed from [it]." Panic-stricken, she rushed back "to Simon Peter and the other disciple, the one whom Jesus loved," and told them, "They have taken the Lord out of the tomb, and we do not know where they have laid him." Peter and the other disciple ran to the tomb, and actually went into it, first Peter, then the other disciple; and this other disciple, on going inside the tomb, "saw" what Peter had seen — a tomb empty except for the linen shroud in which Jesus had been wrapped and the cloth that had been on his head.

The gospel says that the beloved disciple saw these things "and believed." Believed what? That Jesus had been raised from the dead? Well, no; because the evangelist immediately added that Peter and the other disciple "as yet did not understand the scripture, that Jesus must rise from the dead." So when the disciple "saw and believed," what was it that he believed? It must have been Mary Magdalene's report — that "they (whoever *they* were) had taken the Lord out of the tomb," that the corpse of Jesus was indeed gone. And what did they make of the fact? They shrugged their shoulders and "returned to their homes."

Taken by itself, then, the empty tomb is unfinished evidence. It tells us only one thing — that on the morning of the third day after Jesus died and was buried, his corpse was gone from the tomb where it had been laid. And that is where the puzzle *begins*, not where it ends; it is the fact that prompts the investigation into the mystery, not the fact that solves the mystery. For the empty tomb, by itself, does not "prove" that Jesus has been raised from the dead and is alive; it only shows that he is not there.

Thus we are thrown back upon the testimony of Mary Magdalene, Simon Peter, "and the other disciple, the one whom Jesus loved." So far, their testimony has not been very promising: the only thing we learn from them is the fact that the body of Jesus is gone and the tomb is empty. And yet, unpromising as this may be in terms of reaching a solution, their testimonies are all the more credible for being the witness of three people who are dismayed, grieved, and above all puzzled by what they have seen. Mary Magdalene's report to Peter and the other disciple did not presume resurrection or any other kind of supernatural intervention. On the contrary, Mary was presuming what we would presume — that the world was still functioning according to the laws of nature as we know them. Which is to say, Jesus was dead; and since he was dead, but his body was missing, some other human being must have taken it. We are talking about grave-robbing here. For that very reason, Peter and the other disciple were unwilling to believe Mary's report; and so they ran to see for themselves. Seeing is believing; the tomb was indeed as empty, Jesus' body was indeed gone, as Mary had said; so they believed her report — and were just as puzzled by the evidence as she.

Peter and the other disciple went home; Mary stayed at the tomb, and gave vent to her grief. After a while, her sobbing abated, and she wiped her eyes. Tears still rolled down her cheeks, but she could at least see; so she stooped down and peered inside the tomb, just to have another look. No doubt she blinked, and blinked again, for she saw two figures in white, sitting where the body of Jesus had been lying. "They said to her, 'Woman, why are you weeping?' " The gospel says that these two figures were angels, but even so Mary did not twig to the significance of their being there. She simply repeated the likeliest explanation she could think of: "she said to them, 'They have taken away my Lord, and I do not know where they have laid him.' " Then it happened. Mary stood up, turned around, and found another figure standing there. It was Jesus, "but she did not know that it was Jesus"; she thought he was the gardener or caretaker. "Jesus said to her, 'Woman, why are you weeping? Whom are you looking for?' Mary said to him, 'Sir, if you have carried him away, tell me where you have laid him, and I will take him away.' Jesus said to her, 'Mary!' She turned and said to him in Hebrew, 'Rabbouni!' (which means Teacher)." Jesus gave her a message to deliver to the disciples; then Mary ran back into the city and "announced to the disciples, 'I have seen the Lord!' "

Mary Magdalene was not the only person that the risen Lord appeared to; but Mary was the first. And just as the disciples had learned to trust her testimony about the empty tomb, so now they trusted her announcement that she had seen Jesus — not his dead body, but Jesus himself, risen from the dead and alive. Mary Magdalene was the apostle to the apostles, and by her apostleship to them, they became apostles of the risen Lord Jesus to us.

We believe in the resurrection, not because we ourselves have seen the risen Lord, but because we believe and trust the testimony of others — the testimony of Mary Magdalene, of Simon Peter and the beloved disciple, of the other apostles, of Paul, and of all who have handed on their witness from one generation to another, down to us. And we accept that witness, not because we can check the physical facts for ourselves, but because we know those who have told us and have known them to be trustworthy. A community does not survive on the basis of physical proof, and a community whose members do not trust each other unless and until each person's testimony can be verified, is a community which will soon fail. The Church is no exception; and that is why the Church calls for us to live by faith — not only by faith in the invisible God, but also by faith in each other's testimony to what this God has done.

Of course, that requires that each of us be truthful — and trustworthy — to one another. The first generation of the Church believed in the resurrection of Jesus because they found they could trust those who had seen the Lord Jesus after he rose from the dead. The character of Mary Magdalene, of Peter and the beloved disciple, of Paul and James and John, of Mary, the mother of Jesus, and James his brother was their oath, and the proof of their testimony was the way they lived. For they staked their lives on the resurrection, and acted accordingly.

So with us. We need to accept the witness of Mary Magdalene and the apostles, of the Church, and of each other in the Church — and to stake our lives on the resurrection, as they did, by living in accordance with the life of Jesus and the love of the God who raised him from the dead.

Turning Around

She turned around and saw Jesus standing there.

(JOHN 20:14A)

For our paschal lamb, Christ, has been sacrificed.

(1 CORINTHIANS 5:7)

When I turned thirty-five — and I won't tell you how many years ago *that* was — my wife, Mary, was nice enough to throw a big birthday party for me. As many of you know, I am not a party animal; but this was just the kind of party I like — good friends, a lovely meal, and lively conversation. Indeed, the party came together so nicely, the feeling in our living room was so mellow, that about an hour into the event it occurred to me: this really is as good as it gets. This thought passed through my mind, paused, liked what it saw, and settled in for the duration. But of course, all good things must come to an end; and part of the goodness of truly good things is that everybody knows when it is time to go. And that is just what happened, some three hours later; the guests began to make their departure. At one point the stream of departures came to a brief halt, and one of the guests and I found ourselves lingering at the door while Mary and his wife chatted merrily for a bit longer. While we were standing there, this guest more or less spoke into the air and said, "So, you're thirty-five! Well, you know, this is the age they say you're at your peak." Then he turned to me. "Just remember, it's all downhill from here."

I wish I could say that my life since that thirty-fifth birthday has proved him wrong; but there are moments, which seem to be occurring with increasing frequency, when I have to admit that the old grey mare, she ain't what she used to be. I happen to be one of those people whose hair doesn't turn grey in great swaths; I've noticed a few strands at the temple, but for the rest it looks as if I'll be like my grandfather O'Brien, whose hair did not turn white or even grey so much as become a more and more washed-out brown. But if my grandfather's hair did not turn grey, his complexion certainly did. That's great, I think, just great: I have the genes of a man who for the last twenty years of his life looked like wrinkled putty.

I suppose all this should make me face each new birthday with the cheer of someone serving a life sentence at Kingston Penitentiary, with no hope of parole. Curiously enough, though, birthdays and their reminder that you're another year older and deeper in debt, don't really bother me. I may not be a party animal, but I do like a party once in a while, especially when it's for me. No, if I have any trouble with going downhill since the age of thirty-five, it is usually at this time of year, at Easter. And it is not just because the week between Palm Sunday and today is always the busiest season for a parson, bar none. It's also, and much more, because of what Easter is supposed to mean.

We celebrate this day for one reason, to rejoice in one terrific fact: Jesus lives. He who was done to death on a cross three days ago, today is alive again. Alive again, not just in the sense of a resuscitated corpse, not just in the sense that he was granted a reprieve from death, nor in the sense that his life has been

142   Christ Our Passover

recycled. Something far greater happened today. For the life that Jesus now has is a genuinely new life. This one man's mortality has been turned around, changed, converted, so that the humanity of Jesus now *actively* shares in the divinity of God. And just as that is the meaning of Easter, so it is the meaning of salvation altogether: that human nature should become a participant of the divine nature (2 Peter 1:4).

In today's gospel we heard how Mary Magdalene was alone in the garden where Jesus had been buried; she was weeping because Jesus' body was gone, and she did not know where. Then she heard the sound of two voices asking her what her tears were about, and "she turned around and saw Jesus standing there." In the ancient tongues of the Bible, Mary Magdalene *converted* and saw Jesus standing there. For that is what conversion basically means — a turning around, a change of direction. So when Mary turned around, her life was converted to Jesus' life. Not just in the sense that she changed her lifestyle; no, the change went infinitely deeper — she was turned, changed, converted to share in the life of him who is himself the union of our humanity and God's glory. On this Easter morning, Mary Magdalene became the first to know the conversion that St. Paul spoke of in today's epistle: "As all die in Adam, so all will be made alive in Christ." We shall all turn around, as Mary did, and each one of us will be converted from the humanity of Adam to the new, the risen-again humanity of Jesus.

But this is where the old grey mare that ain't what she used to be sometimes has trouble generating the juices of Easter joy. The only conversion most of us feel most of the time is a conversion to more of the same. We're certainly changing, as our bodies get older, but it isn't by turning around; it seems to be only a matter of rolling further down the downhill track, and being deflected from our path by bumping into things that may stop us until we can be repaired and then continue rolling downhill. There is a hymn that has us sing,

> Easter triumph, Easter joy,
> this alone can sin destroy.

Well, maybe; but just growing grey can take the wind out of "Easter triumph, Easter joy," even before we sin.

But perhaps the problem is not the gap between the ordinary life we know and the joy we are supposed to feel at Easter. Perhaps the real problem is the gap we let open between the pains of Good Friday and the glory of today, Easter Day. For the truth is, Easter Day does not stand in a separate compartment all by itself, apart from the compartment of Good Friday. Together, they form a single feast, the feast of our passover. And passover marks a passage, a passing over from one state or condition into another. That is why we hail Jesus in the liturgy, at the breaking of the bread, with the words: "Christ our Passover has been sacrificed for us." Jesus *passed over* from death to the glory of God's eternal life; and that makes him — that makes his whole person — *the* Passover. But he is the passover, our passover, by virtue of his whole passage, his whole movement from Friday to Sunday. And this means that, even as we celebrate his resurrection today, we must not forget, we must keep clearly in view, his death three days ago. The resurrection he knew today did not cancel out his crucifixion, but fulfilled it; and the passover he underwent did not erase the pains of Good Friday so much as reveal the purpose of those pains. Remember, his risen body still bore the marks of the nails and the spear when he appeared to his disciples this morning — "those wounds," a hymn says, which are "yet visible above / In beauty glorified." Jesus conquered death by passing *through* death, not by avoiding it; and he redeemed the pains of our humanity by carrying their marks over into the resurrection, not by shedding them along the way.

There's a saying that I'm not especially fond of: "It's the journey, not the arrival, that matters." Poppycock, I would normally say; so far as I'm concerned, travelling is nothing but one big pain in the neck, and arriving is a vast relief. But Easter is the one occasion when there's some truth to the saying. For the passover-journey from the crucifixion on Good Friday matters at least as much as the arrival at the resurrection on Easter Day. For Easter is the reason for Good Friday, even as Good Friday is the reason for Easter.

That is why we have been baptized, and why we share the eucharist, which is our passover-banquet: So that we may join in the passover of the One who is "our Passover." For "if we have been united with him in a death like his, we will certainly be united with him in a resurrection like his." That is St. Paul speaking; and his words refer to a passover, a passing-over that we ourselves are now engaged in. The Son of God took our lot, our condition, so seriously that he was willing to endure all the pains and terrors of our humanity; and that means, he redeems us from our pains *through* our pains. If we are united with him, he is also united with us. He joins us in the pains of our own passages through this life, so that he might convert that passage into a passover and turn us from mere mortals into sharers of the glory of God.

Easter Season

BELIEVING

The other disciples told [Thomas], "We have seen the Lord."
But he said to them, "Unless I see the mark of the nails in his
hands, and put my finger in the mark of the nails and my
hand in his side, I will not believe."

(JOHN 20:25)

I have A very modern disease, one that (I'm told) afflicts
especially males. It's not a life-threatening disease, unless
the wife of the male who suffers from it is finally driven over
the edge by its symptoms and murders her spouse. I suspect,
though, that a jury of such a woman's peers would return a
verdict of justifiable homicide. For the condition I'm talking
about is The TV Converter Syndrome. It's that disease that
makes someone sit in a chair before the television, with the TV
guide on his lap, open to that night's listings, and the converter
in his hands. The converter is pointed at the television, and
though the sufferer of TV Converter Syndrome has thoroughly
researched the night's programs in the guide on his lap, he still
presses the up button, blipping through all the channels till he
gets to the upper limit of available stations — and then moves
his thumb over to the down button, and begins blipping through
all the channels again until he reaches the lower limit of available stations. Every now and again the TV Converter
Syndromidary will pause, usually not to watch a program but a
commercial; then, when the commercial is over, he resumes

clicking and blipping up or down the channels. This is the modern disease that I suffer; and it is no consolation that millions of other North American males, and a few thousands of females, also suffer it.

Earlier this past week I had a particularly bad case of TV Converter Syndrome, what you might call a converter bender. I don't know why I spent a full ninety minutes clicking and blipping up and down the channels, pausing nowhere for more than ninety seconds; maybe it was post-Holy Week/Easter fatigue. Anyway, there I was, sitting downstairs in front of the television, with the TV guide on my lap, fully cognizant of what was on — which was precisely nothing — and yet click-click-clicking up and down, down and up the dial. At some point thumb fatigue set in, and I let the television stay on one of those merchandising channels where a perky young woman talks to a stolid middle-aged woman about the virtues of some product or other. I forget what the product was in this particular case; all I remember is that the claims the perky woman made for the product seemed — shall we say? — unrealistic. Maybe I was just tired, but I watched this promotion with a jaundiced attitude. The perky woman finished her perky presentation, and I heard myself mutter, "Ha! Seeing is believing, sweetheart."

The next morning I was in a far better mood; I was beginning to feel like Easter again, so I read the readings for today, to prepare for the sermon I would have to deliver. And there was the gospel we have just heard. Jesus had risen from the dead and appeared to ten of the remaining eleven of his disciples. Judas Iscariot, the one who had betrayed Jesus, was not there, as was only to be expected; but the disciple named Thomas had also been absent, for whatever reason. He came back from wherever he was, and the others told him, "We have seen the Lord!" He responded, "Unless I see the mark of the nails in his hands, and put my finger in the mark of the nails and my hand in his side, I will not believe." In other words, seeing is believing, sweetheart.

Now, it occurs to me that Thomas's scepticism was a lot like the attitude I had that evening when I suffered my TV Converter Syndrome bender. I wonder if he was not suffering from the kind of fatigue that always follows a week full of stresses and strains, the sort of fatigue that makes you — not exactly bored but ... dulled. People tell you things, but you can't or won't take them in. The information doesn't even land on the surface of your mind and bounce off; you simply swat it away like a fly before it lights on you.

A lot of commentators pinpoint this sort of attitude as something specially modern, as a feature peculiar to people of this day and age — as if we were the only people in history ever to have suffered a scepticism that comes not from conviction but from fatigue. Today's gospel gives the lie to that idea. Thomas was worn out by everything that had happened in the previous seven days — Palm Sunday, the crowds, the excitement, then the strangely foreboding supper on Thursday night, followed by the arrest, trial, and execution of his teacher Jesus. Thomas was suffering overload, and he just couldn't or wouldn't take in anything more, unless it hit him right in the face and he had to react. It is a condition that in the Great War was called "shell-shock" and which physicians now call Post-Traumatic Stress Disorder — a psychosomatic response to catastrophe that leaves the sufferer almost totally devoid of energy, in a frame of mind so completely negative that there seems to be nothing in the frame at all; horrified into silence, the sufferer lacks any will to communicate, and can only function under extreme pressure. And that sounds like Thomas's case.

It also sounds like our own. We are a shell-shocked civilization; and with that condition comes the negative attitude, the sceptical frame of mind, whose source is not conviction but fatigue; it is the soul's reaction to an overload of stimulation. We close in on ourselves, the way Thomas did, and make our own private experiences the only test of truth: "Something is not true, unless I myself have seen it and touched it; and even then, it has to come to me, I'm not going to go out of my way to find out if it's real."

The truly damnable thing about this attitude, this frame of mind, this condition, this disease is, that it rots faith. Not just religious faith, but also the elemental faith that allows us to trust one another, to have confidence in each other and each other's word. For that is what lets us get on in the world, or even just to get through each day — our ability to trust one another, to accept as the truth what someone tells us is true even though we ourselves have not seen it, touched it, experienced it. We rely on one another to tell the truth, and on our own faith in one another to know the truth. If, on the contrary, we distrusted everything everybody told us, until we could prove it for ourselves, we would be mired in inaction, incapable of doing anything, thinking anything, knowing anything, loving anything. It is faith, it is believing the word of those whom we trust, that gives us the power to act.

And if that is the case in everyday life, it is also the case in Christian life. For we are here, we are celebrating the resurrection, we are receiving Jesus, the risen Lord, in the sacrament, because we have believed the word of those who have believed the word of Peter, and James, and Andrew, and Paul, and yes, finally, Thomas. For the Lord Jesus had pity on Thomas and gave him just the proof he demanded, the opportunity to see and touch the wounds of crucifixion on Jesus' body. But then the Lord told Thomas that this experience granted him no special privileges. He said, "Have you believed because you have seen me? Blessed are those who have not seen and yet have come to believe" (John 20:29). Thomas had seen the risen Lord, but now it was his duty to go forth and live in such a way that others might trust him — have faith in him and his word — when he proclaimed the good news of the resurrection. For believing the resurrection of Jesus would involve trusting the word of Thomas.

And that is what has gone on ever since — we are the latest generations of Christians who have trusted the word of others, our parents, our relatives, our neighbours, and who knows? maybe even a priest or two, and come to believe the truth of Jesus, the crucified Lord risen again.

Sometimes our enthusiasm may flag, and our willingness to do "the church thing" may become infected with a certain fatigue. That is only human, and I am living proof that it happens to priests as well as to people in the pews. But such flagging of enthusiasm, such weariness with churchiness, is not the same as loss of faith. Faith is the opposite of fatigue, it never suffers the scepticism that attends and animates the TV Converter Syndrome, it is never shell-shocked. For faith attends to others with trust; it believes the word of those others, not out of gullibility, but out of a desire to live and be truly alive. For faith knows that God not only moves in mysterious ways his wonders to perform; God also moves through each of us, to give us the truth of his Son, who is the resurrection and the life, so that we in our turn may live in such a way that those who come after us may believe our word and know the risen Lord too.

BREAKFAST

When [the disciples] had gone ashore, they saw a charcoal fire there, with fish on it, and bread…. Jesus said to them, "Come and have breakfast." Now none of the disciples dared to ask him, "Who are you?" because they knew it was the Lord. Jesus came and took the bread and gave it to them, and did the same with the fish.

(JOHN 21:9, 12–13)

The disciples had spent a hard and thoroughly unproductive night fishing. This was not recreational fishing, fishing for the sport of it; it was their livelihood, the job that let them put bread on their tables and shirts on their backs, keep a roof over their heads, and pay their taxes. So it was a discouraging night's work — until dawn, when Jesus appeared on the shore, called out to them and told them to cast their nets on the other side of the boat. Then they began to haul in the biggest catch any of them had ever seen, and their fishing became really hard work. When they finally went ashore, they saw a charcoal fire there, with fish on it, and bread. And Jesus said to them, "Come and have breakfast"; and he took the bread and gave it to them, and did the same with the fish. That breakfast was a very ordinary meal. A charcoal fire with fish lying on it, and a loaf of bread — after a hard night of fishing, this was the sort of breakfast that Peter and the other disciples would have made for themselves in any case.

That breakfast on the beach was very ordinary in another

sense: sharing a meal with his disciples was the normal way in which the risen Lord appeared to them. As in nearly every other encounter with the risen Lord, so now at the breakfast in Galilee, the disciples knew Jesus "in the breaking of bread." Ordinary, typical, matter of fact — and yet the actual circumstances were none of those things. There was the sudden, net-busting catch of fish, after a long night of fruitless labour; and on shore there was a stranger who was no stranger at all. No one needed to ask this stranger, "Who are you?" They knew it was the Lord. The shape of normal experience remained, and yet was broken open; everyday details suddenly had a special importance, and an ordinary meal was transformed into an extraordinary moment of communion with the One who is the Resurrection and the Life.

And so it is to this day, whenever we celebrate the eucharist. We gather at a table, and we eat ordinary, even rather paltry things — wafers made of flour and water, and wine of a sort that is rough on the palate. But the setting in which we eat these things makes them become strange; and the strangeness of the setting is itself a call to discernment. For just as Peter and the other disciples did on that morning so long ago on the beach in Galilee, so this morning, here in this church, we ourselves share a meal with our risen Lord; and when we share this meal, we share the very life of him who is both a stranger and an intimate. He is a stranger, in that we can never domesticate him in the present order of things, nor reduce him to the normal round of everyday reality. But he is also an intimate, in that he enters the very interstices of our natural lives, to transform, convert, and nourish us for the new life of God's unspeakable glory.

And one thing more. If there is a change in the ordinary things we shall eat and drink at our altars, a change in the bread and the wine we shall receive in this eucharist, that change is geared to the change that God seeks to work in us who eat and drink. The bread and wine are not consecrated for their own sake but for the sake of consecrating us — for the sake of converting us into the image of him who died and was raised again. In thus reshaping us, God does not destroy our humanity and replace it with something else. Instead, the Almighty fulfils our reality so that we may be truly human, human in the way that God has always intended us to be, ever since the beginning of creation. This is the reason for which the bread and wine are consecrated; and this conversion of ordinary human life into true human life is the model and rule for what happens to ordinary bread and wine in this eucharist. These elements do not cease to be what they are; by the all-powerful love of God in Christ, they are converted into what they are most truly meant to be — elements of conviviality with the Creator. We who bear Christ by virtue of our baptism, eat this bread and drink this wine in order to feast with the Lord, with the Lord who is the fullness and fulfilment of our lives — and not only of our lives, but also of the bread and the wine, of the fish and the fire, and of all created things.

May we not fail this moment and the feast we now celebrate; may God the Father, who raised Jesus from the dead, grant us the power and the patience, the faith and the love, to discern his risen Son in the ordinary things we take and bless and eat in the eucharist. And may the same God grant us still greater gifts: the faith and the love to carry this discernment, yes, the power and the patience to carry Jesus himself into the world, into each corner of the world where we live; that we may do God's will and be agents of the conversion that God seeks for all created things — the conversion that does not destroy our reality but brings us to our fullness and our truth by Jesus Christ, the Lord once crucified, now risen, and alive forever.

Shepherd and Sheep

"My sheep hear my voice. I know them, and they follow me. I give them eternal life, and they will never perish. No one will snatch them out of my hand."

(John 10:27–28)

The fourth Sunday of Easter is commonly called "Good Shepherd Sunday," because the gospel always comes from one of those passages where Jesus portrays himself as a shepherd. Or rather, as *the* Shepherd who cares for the flock — the flock that is God's chosen people — and watches over them so diligently, so fiercely, that "no one will snatch them out of [his] hand." And that has made this Sunday a big favourite with many generations of Christians. For the image of Jesus the shepherd, as one who "will gather the lambs in his arms, and carry them in his bosom, and gently lead the mother sheep" (Isaiah 40:11) has made lots of people feel all warm and fuzzy.

I am not one of them. I have always approached this Sunday with a heavy heart, and whenever it has come time to prepare for it, my mind has uttered a little sigh — the sort of sigh you make when, on the whole, you'd rather be doing something else. The sort of sigh that comes out as, "Oh, all right; let's get it over with." The approach of this year's Fourth Sunday of Easter started off no differently, and when I looked up the readings for today, my mind breathed that silent sigh it has always breathed at the prospect of Good Shepherd Sunday.

But then something different did happen. No sooner had I sighed my annual Good Shepherd Sunday sigh, than a question popped into my head — "*Why* does Good Shepherd Sunday make me sigh?" Now, I am not quick on my feet. Ask me a serious question, and my mind tends to go blank at first, not because I'm confused but because, though I live in the computer age and even use a computer, my mind still works at the speed of handwriting — and I do not mean shorthand. I'm one of those people who pieces an answer together over a space of hours or even days — which is why I never think of the snappy comeback to an outrageous comment until several hours after I've left the party. And so it was in this case. *Why* does Good Shepherd Sunday make me sigh? It took me until Thursday evening to put all the pieces of an answer together. And this is what I came up with:

Jesus called himself the Good Shepherd. Okay; but what message is this image sending about *us*? I mean, a shepherd takes care of sheep, right? And sheep are very stupid animals. Not quite the stupidest animals in all of God's good creation, but close to it. They are a notch or two smarter than chickens, which puts them on the same level of intelligence as a dead cow. I don't know about you, but being compared with sheep does not sound to me like very much of a compliment. And that is what I have been fighting, all these years of Good Shepherd Sundays — not the image of Jesus as Good Shepherd, but the image in the background of that image — the image of us as stupid sheep.

One of the things we humans find very hard to do, is to see what's right in front of our noses. Like those really irritating people at a party or a meeting who, while you are talking with them, spend the whole time looking around the room to see who else is there. We all have the difficulty of which these people are the most extreme — and most aggravating — example. We have trouble noticing facts that are in the foreground; instead, we gaze past them, squinting to make out the facts, the figures, the angles, in the background. And that is certainly what I was doing whenever Good Shepherd Sunday rolled around. I was looking at the sheep in the background, not at the Shepherd in the foreground.

And what does the figure of the shepherd stand for? Nurture and protection of those creatures who, without him, would strip a landscape so bare that they would eventually begin to starve themselves; who, without him, would be easy pickings for predators. But the point of today's gospel, the point of Good Shepherd Sunday, is not that we are as stupid as sheep. The point is that we need nurture and protection; we humans need to be taken care of, because we are not very good at taking care of ourselves, and we are easy pickings for our predator, which is death.

It was just this predator that Jesus meant when, in today's gospel, he said that "no one will snatch [any of my flock] out of my hand." For him, death had a double-barrelled meaning and could take place on two levels. The first level was of course the present life we have in this world; and on this level, death means the end of life, or at least of physical life — our bodies shut down, by reason of disease, or because of an acute trauma, or just because they wear out. That's the normal meaning of death. But for Jesus there was another meaning, just as normal and even more total. This is the death of the spirit as well as of the body, where the soul, the living centre of a person, is extinguished — and extinguished forever. This does not happen when the lungs cease breathing and the heart stops and the brain shuts down, at the moment of physical death in time. No, this death occurs in eternity, and it happens when the spirit, the living centre of a person, goes out, like a candle in the wind, because it cannot bear the presence of the glory of God. It is not a question of God snuffing the spirit out; it is a question of a human having lived in such a way that his or her spirit cannot stand the sight of God and disappears in a wisp — forever.

It is this death, eternal death, that will never snatch us out of Jesus' hand; for it is against this death that Jesus himself stands as our shepherd, our guard, our protector. And he seeks to give us pasture, to nourish and sustain us for the very life that is the opposite of eternal death — for the life where our spirits, our living centres, are so strong, so right in themselves, that we shall be able to bear that "eternal weight of glory beyond all measure" (2 Corinthians 4:17), which is the resurrection of our own bodies, and which we shall not only endure but also rejoice and be glad in the breath of the unveiled glory of God. And so the Shepherd feeds us out of his own life, with his own body and blood, to make our lives ready for eternal life. If we receive this mystery so faithfully as to live faithful to God in the world, the Shepherd will lead us into the banquet of glory. Then and there, just as no one was able to snatch us out of his hand, so God will snatch our humanity up into the threefold, single embrace of triune divinity.

THE WORKS
THAT BEAR WITNESS

After this I looked, and there was a great multitude that no one could count, from every nation, from all tribes and peoples and languages, standing before the throne and before the Lamb, robed in white, with palm branches in their hands....
"These are they who have come out of the great ordeal; they have washed their robes and made them white in the blood of the Lamb."

(REVELATION 7:9, 14B)

Jesus answered, "The works that I do in my Father's name testify to me."

(JOHN 10:25B)

The great Lerner and Loewe musical *My Fair Lady* opened on Broadway some forty-five years ago, and since then not a year has passed without a production of the show being mounted somewhere in North America. The reason is not hard to fathom. It almost defines the form of the Broadway musical, with back-to-back "show-stopping" tunes. One of those tunes sticks in my mind right now. It is the one where Eliza Doolittle breaks into exasperated song and says, "Don't talk of love, show me!" Eliza was addressing the fatuous Freddie; but it occurs to me that, since the beginning of time, humans have been addressing the same demand to God. The Scriptures talk a lot about the love that the Almighty has for us; and as often as not our response has been, "Show us!"

The gospels tell us that the leaders of the people levelled this very demand — "Show us!" — at Jesus himself. Time and time again, they came up to him and said, "Show us a sign that will prove that you come from God." Sometimes Jesus replied by denouncing their lack of faith: "Why does this generation ask for a sign?" he said. "Truly I tell you, no sign will be given to this generation" (Mark 8:12). On other occasions, Jesus responded in a rather more subtle way — as, for instance, in today's gospel. There, we are told that the leaders of the people came up to Jesus and said: "How long will you keep us in suspense? If you are the Messiah, tell us plainly." And Jesus replied: "I have told you.... The works that I do in my Father's name testify to me." Jesus had indeed been telling them that he was the Messiah — and had been showing them God's love — only in works, not in words; he had not been talking about it, he had been doing it. And those same works of his bore witness that he and his Father were one. This answer did not satisfy the leaders of the people then, and perhaps it leaves us restless even now.

For what *are* the works that Jesus does in his Father's name? Are they miracles and mighty signs? Perhaps — after all, when John the Baptist sent some of his disciples to ask Jesus: "Are you the one who is to come, or are we to wait for another?" Jesus told them "Go and tell John what you hear and see: the blind receive their sight, the lame walk, the lepers are cleansed, the deaf hear, the dead are raised, and the poor have good news brought to them" (Matthew 11:2–5). That sounds very much as if miracles are indeed the works that testify to the truth that

Jesus is the Messiah. But then again, we must take into account all those times when Jesus denounced the hankering for "mighty signs and wonders" and, on the contrary, testified that the works that bear witness to him can be recognized as such only by those who already believe in him. And if one already believes in him, what miracle could one possibly need to bear witness to him? By the same token, if one does not believe in him, what miracle could possibly do the trick? And so we come back to the problem. If the works that bear witness to Jesus are not (or not *necessarily*) miracles and mighty wonders, what are they?

A hint of the answer may be found in the book of Revelation, where St. John the Divine sees a vision of the end of the ages. In this vision he beholds "a great multitude that no one could count, from every nation, from all tribes and peoples and languages, standing before the throne [of God] and before the Lamb." The Lamb is, of course, Jesus crucified, risen, and now glorified; he is the fullness of God's Passover, who precisely as the paschal Lamb is also the good shepherd guiding his flock, the faithful, across the ocean of death and gathering them in the promised land of eternal life. John's vision, then, is an image of salvation — and salvation is the work that Jesus does. But salvation is always a verb, and it is always a verb with an object. The object of the salvation that Jesus works, is that "great multitude that no one could count," which John beheld in his vision. So, what are the works that Jesus does in the Father's name — the works that testify and bear witness to him? They are nothing other or less than all the people who stand before God. Each and every one of that countless throng is a work of Christ, a mighty deed of his saving power. The true works of Jesus are the people he has redeemed, not miracles; and the company of the redeemed is all the witness he needs to show that he comes from the Father. In other words, there are no other works in witness of Christ but ourselves.

Now, this very thought, when we look around us and when we look at ourselves, might give us pause. Once, during the Napoleonic wars, the Duke of Wellington watched his British troops as they marched by. He turned to a subordinate and said, "I do not know if they frighten the enemy, but by God, Sir, they frighten me!" Christ must sometimes mutter the same thing to the Father, as he watches the Church march by. We who are his works often appear not to have worked out very well.

But our rag-tag appearance, as we go our way wracked by pains and wrecked by pride, afflicted with anxieties and twisted by rage — this rag-tag appearance of ours is not the whole story; for somehow or other, by fits and starts, we do get the job done. We have found the courage of loyalty and the patience of love to continue gathering here Sunday after Sunday. We may not get along with everybody who gathers for worship in this place, but still we gather with each other, thereby acknowledging (sometimes in spite of ourselves) that the others here with us are works of Christ just as much as we are. And here we gather together with hope and faith that the God who baptized each of us into Christ will continue to convert us and shape us as a work of Christ.

So there are no mighty signs and wonders but only ourselves. Or rather, we ourselves are the mighty signs and wonders — we ourselves, and the Christ who is in the midst of us whenever two or three, ten or twenty, fifty or one hundred and fifty, come together in his name. And that is how Christ is now doing his works — in each one of us as individuals, because all of us together are a company and a community that is named with his own name.

And being named with the name of Jesus Christ never ceases to be a community affair. None of us possesses Christ, none of us is a work of Christ, alone and in private. The life that he shares *with* us is a life that he means to be shared *by* us, one with another. We need each other in order to know Christ. Each of us has strengths or talents that may support somebody else in their search for salvation, and each of us also has weaknesses or blind-spots that make us require the assistance of others in order to do what we are called to do and to be. God created a universe of things nearly infinite in their differences; and so it continues in the order of salvation — it is in the sheer diversity of Christ's works that God is magnified. We shall never know Christ unless we are willing to look for him in each other, nor shall we ever share the divine life in common with God unless we are willing to share in common the Christ who is in us with one another. Only thus are we the works of Christ, and only together does he make us true sharers in the multitude of those whom no human can number.

So, the next time the pains of your humanity turn you into Eliza Doolittles and make you cry, "Don't talk of God's love, show me!" — do not look for a miracle, some mighty sign and wonder. Look instead to one another; for together we are the works that show and bear witness to the love of God that is in Christ Jesus our Lord.

THE WAY OF PRUDENCE

We do not want you to be uninformed, brothers and sisters,
about those who have died, so that you may not grieve as
others do who have no hope.

(1 THESSALONIANS 4:13)

This is a dark time for us, a season of sorrow within the
Easter season, when the Church is supposed to be rejoicing and singing Alleluia. It reminds me of another dark time,
the season of Advent, when night falls early and swiftly. It is a
time when few people come out for evening services; they hurry
home, or they hurry downtown to finish their Christmas shop-
ping. In the years that I was a priest in this parish, I can
remember several times in the last week of Advent when only
two people showed up for Evening Prayer — myself, and Prudence Tracy. I was there because the rector had appointed me
to celebrate the evening mass at 6:00 o'clock; Prudence was
there to worship God — and then, most often, to stay on and
finish the Sunday bulletin.

Evening Prayer in Advent is fairly ordinary, without anything special, until the seventeenth of December; and then the
Church ordains a sequence of seven antiphons, one each day,
to be said with the Magnificat, an evening canticle that is said
after the first reading from Scripture. On 17 December, the
proper antiphon goes this way: "O Wisdom, you came forth
from the mouth of the Most High, and reach from one end of

the earth to the other, mightily and sweetly ordering all things: Come and teach us the way of prudence." Whenever we said this antiphon, a small burble of laughter would rise from the pew where Prudence sat; and after Evening Prayer she used to joke how complimented she felt, that the Church should pray for wisdom to come and teach us her way, "the way of Prudence."

Prudence has now gone her way — too soon, much too soon, for us. And though none of us can have wished for her to endure any longer the agonies she bore in these last two years, simply that we might continue to enjoy the pleasure of her company; yet we do miss her, and feel the pain of no longer having her with us, and grieve that, before we were ready to let her go, she was subjected to the dominion of our final enemy, death. She has gone from us; and yet our prayer is still, now more than ever, that Wisdom will indeed come and teach us the way of Prudence.

Such a prayer might appear to be asking for retrospective powers, for the gift of remembrance — a remembrance of Prudence just sharp enough to let us recall the look in her eyes and the sound of her laughter on this or that occasion; but also a remembrance just fuzzy enough to let us forget that we shall have no more living occasions to see her eyes or hear her laughter again in this world. That would be a task difficult enough in itself; but other difficulties crop up as well. Not the least of them is the role of the preacher. For why should the preacher presume upon the pulpit and make his own remembrance of the way of Prudence privileged above the remembrances that the rest of you have? For the way of Prudence, her path through this world, abounded in intersections; she made her life a place where religion, literature, music, business, and scholarship all met. Her spirit became a chamber where St. Benedict and

George Herbert and Erasmus rubbed shoulders with Jessye Norman and the films of Merchant and Ivory; and her heart was a neighbourhood in which Kalamazoo, Edinburgh, Oxford, and Port Maitland, Nova Scotia, all stood next-door to the rich silences and baroque exasperations of an Anglo-catholic parish. Who can do justice to the whole of such a life, and whose remembrance can comprehend in a single glance all the variety of Prudence's way? Anecdotes may remind us of the pleasure of her company, but we would need a whole library of anecdotes to approximate the fullness of her presence; and even then, can we be sure that wisdom would have taught us the way of someone so frank and so gracious, and yet so reserved, as Prudence was?

So, when we pray for wisdom to teach us the way of Prudence, perhaps we need to look beyond mere remembrance. It may be that this present service can provide the perspective of wisdom that we seek. For here we celebrate the mystery of God, the God once crucified and now risen, as much as we grieve the death of Prudence. And that is just as Prudence wanted it — I venture to say, just as Prudence wants it even now. For her way brought her to this church every Sunday and nearly every weekday, to celebrate the mystery of God not only through the daily offices of prayer, but also through the mass, as a member of the congregation, as a reader and server, as a master of ceremonies, and latterly as a subdeacon. And so, because of the God to whom this mass bears witness and offers worship, perhaps we must say that the way of Prudence continues, though now beyond our present sight. For since the way of Prudence was to celebrate the mystery of God, perhaps the true remembrance of her is to look beyond this moment and follow the way of Prudence as it rises without end into the God whose own way is infinite.

A high call indeed! — and a call that, I admit, may be heard either as harsh Catholic ideology or as foolish Christian piety in the face of this death and the grief it has caused us. But the call to remember that the way of Prudence was a path of faith, and that this path now converges with the infinite way of the God who is not God of the dead but of the living — such a call is not a demand that we cease to mourn or that we pretend never to feel rage at what appears to be yet another victory for our enemy, death. It is simply an appeal that we ponder the wisdom of the way of Prudence.

Part of that wisdom is the advice that St. Paul addressed to the Christians of Thessalonica, when he told them: "We do not want you to be uninformed, brothers and sisters, about those who have fallen asleep, so that you may not grieve as others do who have no hope."

So that you may not grieve as others do who have no hope. At first hearing, the Apostle seems to be telling us not to grieve at all; mourning (he seems to be saying) is only for unbelieving outsiders, not for true insiders such as "we" are. But I am not sure that this is indeed what Paul meant us to hear. He may not have intended to pose a straightforward contest between unbelievers and believers, between mourners and those who, because of their faith, are incapable of mourning. The real comparison is between kinds of mourning, both of which share the same reason, the loss of someone loved and honoured. But the mourning that Paul calls for, the sort of grieving that the Apostle considers faithful to God, is mourning with hope. It is not that believers deny or do not feel the pain of loss; on the contrary, they feel it and acknowledge its force all the more, because they are believers in the living God, who did not abandon Jesus to the grave nor let his Holy One see corruption (Psalm 16:10; Acts 2:27, 31). For this very reason Christians grieve with hope;

and though their hearts are wrenched with frustrated love and their nerves go numb with something like dread, yet their grief does not master their faith, and their sorrow is oddly open-ended.

Our sorrow is open-ended, but not in the sense that it stretches into eternity; nor do I mean that our grief will simply peter out and no longer hurt as much. The wounds of crucifixion remain on the risen Jesus, and the welts of death still mark the Lord in glory. Just so, the love that makes us grieve will never leave us: it will plead for us at the final judgement; and the invisible marks of our mourning will never be eradicated: they will be touched by the finger of the risen Word made flesh. We may ask that God will remember our sins no more against us; we do not ask that God will let us forget our love, or let us put away the wisdom that taught us to rejoice in the way of Prudence.

Prudence is gone from us, to our grief; but as we pray that God may give us Wisdom to come and teach us the way of Prudence, so Prudence herself may pray to the same God that our grief may learn how to dwell in hope. Thus, even now, we shall continue to join her in celebrating the mystery of God, who flung open the grave and gate of death, that Jesus might be the way of life for all of us who, even as we go down to the dust, sing in the midst of grief this one song of hope: Alleluia, alleluia, alleluia.

THE WAY

(JOHN 14:6)

St. John the evangelist pondered the mystery of salvation, and as he did so he heard Jesus speak these words: "I am the way, and the truth, and the life. No one comes to the Father except through me." This saying reminds us of our goal, the goal of being a Christian, the reason why we were baptized, and the reason why we celebrate and receive this sacrament today. It is simply this: to come to the Father. Salvation is not a thing, but a person, the Father who eternally begets the Word; and the way to the Father is not an abstract principle or a set of rules or a spiritual technique, but another person; for the way to the Father is none other than the very Word who eternally proceeds from the Father.

There you have the gospel, and the Christian faith, all in a nutshell; and perhaps I should not need to say anything more to you or to myself, for I have just spoken what every Christian should know as a matter of course. But you and I are not only Christians; we are also busy human beings, humans whose business with God is too often cluttered up by other business; and so from time to time you and I need to recollect ourselves and remind our hearts of what we are about when we gather here to celebrate the eucharist. It is simply to receive the way to the Father, and to taste the Word, the Son: "For in him all the fullness of God was pleased to dwell" (Colossians 1:19).

And who is this person, this Word, this Son? I have already said what the Church confesses, that he is eternally begotten of the Father; God from God, light from light, true God from true God, of one being with the Father. That is how he exists in deity; but that is not how he is our way to the Father. He is our way to the Father only as the One who came down from heaven, received flesh from the Virgin Mary, and was made a human being; who was crucified and killed, buried, yes, and was raised again as a human being. In all this he was still the Son of God, still the eternally begotten of the Father, in whom all the fullness of God delighted to dwell; and yet he was also the child of Mary, a human being begotten in time, in whom all the fullness of our humanity was embraced by God. And it is through his humanity that this same incarnate Son, Jesus Christ, has become the way to the Father.

For we must recall that salvation is relation to a person, the person whom Jesus knew and named as "Father." And how do we enter personal relations with one another? Only when we can recognize a kinship with someone else, only when we discover some point of contact, some doorway or window by which we may enter into their lives and they may enter into our lives — a gesture, a smile, a word, a sudden discovery that this other person shares something of your own background and interests. And that is just how the person of the Father reaches out to us, to enter into our lives that we may enter into the life of God — the point of contact between us is the humanity of the incarnate Word. His human gestures are the gestures of God; his human smile is the smile of God, his human tears are the tears of the Almighty, and by his history among us we discover the Creator of all sharing the background and interests of our created lives.

We find our way to the Father through the humanity, even the flesh and blood, of Jesus Christ; and by receiving the flesh and blood of this Son, we also receive his union with the Father. We are drawn into that union, made partakers and partners in that union, where Father and Son breathe the one Spirit; where the Son lives into the Father and the Father lives into the Son.

Such is the way of salvation, through the human being of the Son of God to the divine being of Jesus Christ in union with the Father. And such too is the salvation we Christians look for, by baptism, by eucharist, by prayer, and by faith — that we may share the presence of the Father with the Son, whom the Father has shared with us — and even now is pleased to share with us in the bread and wine of the eucharist.

THE VINE
AND THE BRANCHES

I am the true vine, and my Father is the vinegrower…. Abide in me as I abide in you. Just as the branch cannot bear fruit by itself unless it abides in the vine, neither can you unless you abide in me. I am the vine, you are the branches. Those who abide in me and I in them bear much fruit, because apart from me you can do nothing.

(JOHN 15:1, 4–5)

God is love, and those who abide in love abide in God and God abides in them. Love has been perfected among us in this.

(1 JOHN 4:16B, 17A)

What does it mean to be *Christian*? Not an Anglican Christian, or a Roman Catholic Christian, or a Lutheran Christian, or indeed any other brand of Christian, but just Christian — what C. S. Lewis once called "mere Christianity"? Lewis himself gave a highly detailed answer, by way of explaining those teachings that most Christian churches hold in common. He certainly did not produce a "dumbed down" version of the Christian faith, but Lewis's approach was still little more than a variant on the lowest common denominator. And I suspect that most of us would instinctively adopt the same approach, if we were ever asked to say what it means to *be Christian*. Not all of us — well, hardly any of us —— would think to talk, as Lewis did, about the doctrines that most churches hold in common; not out of ignorance of those doctrines, but simply because we sense that doctrines breed controversy — and controversy, we think, is the enemy of "mere Christianity." So we keep mum about such things as God, Christ, the Holy Spirit, baptism, the eucharist, and the Bible, and talk instead about being kind and generous and helpful; we might even say something about being moral, except that we would then get into issues on which all Christians most emphatically do not agree, such as same-sex relationships. Best to play it safe, and stick with kindness, generosity, and helpfulness. The problem is, we may feel vaguely dissatisfied with such an answer to the question of being Christian. Not only have we banished the very particulars that make us want to be Christian; we have also turned Christianity itself into a Happy Face, and its creed into "Have a nice day!"

So again I ask, What does it mean to be *Christian*? To answer the question this time around, perhaps we should look not for the lowest but for the highest common denominator. And just what might that be? Today's gospel gives us a hint. St. John the evangelist, pondering the mystery of Christ, heard Jesus say, "I am the true vine, and my Father is the vinegrower.... You are the branches.... Abide in me as I abide in you." The vine and its branches — we are not dealing with a statement of fact, of course; we are called to ponder an image or, perhaps better said, a metaphor. Jesus does not mean that he *is* a vine or that we *are* branches; he means that the relationship between his life and our lives *acts like* the relation between a vine and its branches. Which is to say, we derive life and sustenance from him; and just as a branch is able to bear fruit only so long as it is attached to the vine, so we are able to do good only so long as we are attached to Jesus.

The metaphor sounds verdant, and might make us think green and leafy thoughts in happy anticipation of the wine that all those clusters of succulent grapes will give us. And indeed, when the ancient Hebrews wanted an idea of what happiness and success were like, they imagined a householder sitting in a vineyard, under the shade of the vines, calm and prosperous in the afternoon heat. But the metaphor in today's gospel is not really all that leafy or succulent. It speaks of vine and branches — of wood that must be strong and hard enough to bear all its offshoots, and of tendrils that must be sinewy enough to hold all those grapes. The metaphor has no time for the mellow contentment of a summer afternoon's wine-tasting party; it is about the basics of viniculture — and thus about the essentials of discipleship. John's gospel never resorts to warm-and-fuzzies, least of all in this metaphor of the vine and its branches. It does not call us to wine-warmed smiles at the sweetness of life; it calls us to ponder the source of our life and the sustenance of our actions, which is simply and only Jesus himself.

The metaphor recognizes no split between religious behaviour and everyday attitudes, between spirituality and what we are pleased (or deluded) to call "real life"; it is frankly stating that our very being comes from, and depends upon, Jesus. But how is this so? In what sense does Jesus act like a vine in relation to us branch-like disciples? It sounds like nonsense; for we start from our individual selves, and view our relation with Jesus as an external commitment. The metaphor reverses that perspective; but on what grounds?

Remember how the gospel, the metaphor, began. Jesus opened his discourse by saying, "I am the true vine, and my Father is the vinegrower.... You are the branches." There are in fact three metaphors at work in this passage: the metaphor of Jesus himself as "the true vine," the metaphor of his disciples as the branches of the true vine, and the metaphor of the one he called "Father" as "the vinegrower." This third metaphor almost immediately disappears from the discourse; it is pursued for a single verse more, and then dropped. But it sets the context of the whole passage; and the context is heavenly. Or rather, not heavenly, so much as cosmic. John's gospel sees the relation of Jesus and the One he calls Father through the lens of Easter Day. So when the gospel speaks of vine and branches, it is not talking about a relationship in the present order of creation; it is talking about a relationship that exists in the order of the new creation — in the new order of reality already inaugurated by the resurrection of Jesus.

Baptism engrafted us into Jesus, the true Vine; and it is baptism that now makes the difference for us. Our life is no longer derived simply from Adam and Eve, that is, from the old order of creation. It has been transformed and converted, so that our root is not in the earth but in the resurrection, or rather in him who is the Resurrection, in Jesus.

This is where the references to the Father come in, the Father who is "the vinegrower," who prunes the branches. For there is a condition to the life that we now live, the new life of the resurrection. The branches of the vine must indeed bear fruit, for "[by this is my Father glorified], that you bear much fruit and become my disciples." And if a branch does not bear fruit, that person "is thrown away like a branch and withers; such branches are gathered, thrown into th fire, and burned."

Now, what kind of fruit are we expected to bear? Well, a branch bears fruit according to the kind of vine it belongs to. Grapes do not grow on pumpkin vines, and pumpkins do not grow on tomato plants. So, we who are branches of Christ the true vine should bear the fruit of Christ. But again I ask, What is the fruit of Christ?

Today's second reading will help — the reading from the First Letter of John. We heard it say: "Beloved, let us love one another, because love is of God; eveyone who loves is born of God and knows God.... God is love.... If we love one another, God lives in us, and his love is perfected in us." Love, *mutual* love, is the fruit of Christ. We are not talking about sexual love, nor are we even talking about sentimental affection. We are talking about another, a third and hardier kind of love.

A while ago I saw a cartoon. It showed a married couple facing one another, and the man was saying to the woman, "Do you think it's possible to love someone you don't like?" The Christian answer is a firm and very unsentimental "Yes." It sometimes occurs to me (and maybe the same thought has occurred to you too) that God really doesn't like us; but then it also occurs to me that we are not very likeable, either as a race of creatures or as individuals. Still, though God may not like us, yet God certainly does love us, "for God *is* love." And "in this is love, not that we loved God but that he loved us and sent his Son to be the atoning sacrifice for our sins" (1 John 4:10).

Or put it this way: God sent the only Son into the world to assume and bear our burden for us. Once planted in our midst, Christ the true vine and resurrection began to transform this creation, so that we who have been born of him through the waters of baptism might be stretched out over the new creation, like boughs over a flourishing garden. And even as the true vine grows into the new earth of the heavenly vinegrower, so are we called to bear one another's burdens in the common life of the redeemed vineyard. This is what it means to love, to bear fruit and to abide as branches in the one true vine, Jesus Christ. It means a certain patience and, more, a certain willing submission to the true needs that another person has, in his or her life in Christ. It means an interlocking of branches, not that we might choke one another off, but that we might support one another as each strives to bring forth Christ.

I said that when the ancient Hebrews imagined what true happiness and success were like, they imagined someone sitting in a vineyard, under the shade of the vines, calm and prosperous in the afternoon heat. And such is what today's gospel asks us to imagine what "the new heavens and the new earth" are like. Only, it is not the happiness of some human on a hillside in Palestine that is at stake. It is the happiness, the blessedness of God almighty. We are called to live in Christ, and to have Christ live in us, and by that very fact to bear such fruit that the Father in heaven might sit in the shade of Christ the vine, under Christ's branches, ourselves, as we sway and spangle in the calm motion of the Spirit.

THE HOLY CITY

And in the spirit [one of the seven angels] carried me away to a great, high mountain and showed me the holy city Jerusalem coming down out of heaven from God. It has the glory of God and a radiance like a very rare jewel, like jasper, clear as crystal. It has a great, high wall with twelve gates, and at the gates twelve angels, and on the gates are inscribed the names of the twelve tribes of the Israelites.... And the wall of the city has twelve foundations, and on them are the twelve names of the twelve apostles of the Lamb.

(REVELATION 21:10–12, 14)

S ome years ago now Mary and I attended a dinner party on a Saturday night. Not the best night for a priest to go out, but it is occasionally useful for clergy to see that there are other ways to spend a Saturday evening besides writing a sermon. In any case, I put on a regular shirt and tie, and off we went to our friends' house. They had no connection with the parish I was then serving; Mary knew them through the choir she had joined. The party turned out to be a much larger affair than we had expected; and apart from our hosts, I knew and was known to no one else. Things went along pleasantly until our host blurted out that I should know something about strange jobs, since I was an Anglican clergyman. He smiled around a room that had suddenly gone stiff with silence. It was as if Newfoundland were in an occupied country, and my host had cheerfully announced that I was a major in the Secret Police.

Then a young man, sitting across from me, broke the very uncomfortable silence. Looking at the floor, he said: "I wonder, how can you believe in all that stuff? You must have a big imagination." People laughed at that, and the party regained its mellowness.

It is true, what that young man said: we Christians do indeed have a big imagination — though not in the sense that he meant. Society assumes that imagination makes things up, that it produces figments, fictions, and illusions. Whereas the Church knows that imagination is the faculty that allows us to recognize images of the invisible in visible things, and to see likenesses of the God who is Spirit in the things of this physical world. We are people with an imagination because images are the only way that creatures of flesh and blood can think, and talk about, and pray to the unseeable Trinity whose own reality makes all else real.

Nowhere in Holy Scripture is this fact more evident than in the very last book of the Bible, the Revelation to John. It is a strange book, in which a Christian prophet named John recounted the visions he was given to see; visions of the end of all things, visions of war in heaven, of the last judgement, and of the final triumph of God and Christ the Lamb. In the climactic vision of the whole book, the culminating image of "what is and what is to come," we catch a glimpse of the Christian imagination at work. For in that vision we are given an image of the final reality, a likeness of the goal to which all things are being brought. An angel shows St. John, and St. John shows us, "the holy city, new Jerusalem, coming down out of heaven from God."

"New Jerusalem" ... John did not envision the kingdom of heaven as a field, the way Jesus did in his parables, nor even as a leafy, frolicsome countryside, the way our great- and great-great-grandparents did. No; John's vision of the new creation is that of a well-built city teeming with people, a city to which all the nations of the earth will come, bringing whatever made them great and powerful as tribute to the ruler of this city, Christ the Lamb. Only, the city that John envisions is not like the cities we know, say, Toronto or Montreal, Halifax or Vancouver. New Jerusalem is like the cities of the Roman empire that John knew. These cities were each a compact little world, small in size, densely populated, and surrounded by a stout wall to keep out wild animals and brigands and to withstand siege by enemies of the empire.

When St. John was inspired to imagine the new creation that is and that is yet to come, he did not draw on some generic, no-name image of a "typical" ancient city. He imagined Jerusalem, the city of David, the site of the holy temple of God, and the place where Jesus was crucified and raised again. And he imagined this same city made totally new. It was not just Jerusalem that he saw in his vision; it was the *new* Jerusalem. And here he drew on a much earlier vision, a prophecy already ancient when St. John wrote his book. It was a vision seen by the Hebrew prophet Isaiah, who then announced what he had been given to see to the people of Jerusalem of his own day, and said:

> Nations shall come to our light,
> and kings to the brightness of your dawn....
>
> Your gates shall always be open;
> day and night they shall not be shut....
>
> They shall call ou the City of the Lord,
> the Zion of the Holy One of Israel....
>
> You shall call your walls Salvation,
> and your gates Praise.

The sun shall no longer be your ight by day,
nor your brightness shall the moon give light to you
by night;

but the Lord will be your everlasting light,
and your God will be your glory."

(ISAIAH 60:3, 11, 14B, 18B–19)

This prophecy of Isaiah is a glorious, gorgeous vision, and it is a vision whose glory is not only undimmed but also renewed in the prophecy of St. John. But one thing would have especially struck both Isaiah's original listeners and John's original readers. Isaiah says that the "gates [of the new Jerusalem] shall always be open; day and night, they shall not be shut." And John says that in his vision he saw a city whose "gates will never be shut by day — and there will be no night there." Indeed, both Isaiah and John go on to say that this city, the new Jerusalem, will be a city without walls — or rather, that its walls will no longer be made of stone and brick; for all the city will have, and all the city will need to surround it, will be the brilliance of the glory of God. And that would have struck Isaiah's contemporaries, and then John's contemporaries some five centuries later, as wonderful — and weird.

For as I said, all ancient cities — and all ancient towns, villages, and hamlets, for that matter — were walled, with gates that were shut and barred at sunset. The ancient world was not a peaceful, settled landscape; it was a world where forests still covered more territory than cultivated land, where wild animals still roamed at large, often straying into the streets and even the houses of large cities; it was a world of robber bands, of villagers marauding another village, their rival, for a well or a field. In short, it was a world of fear, and the walls of a city, a town, or a village, were protection against the fearsome things that helped to make ancient life nasty, brutish, and (above all) short. A wall thus looked to ancient people not only as a protection against nature but also as a necessity of nature. And here was John proclaiming a day when all creation would be gathered into the new Jerusalem, and nature would not need the necessity of walls.

We do not lived in a walled-in world anymore. On the contrary, our cities sprawl and sprawl, so that it is hard to tell where one ends and the next begins. This wall-lessness, this habit of not dwelling behind ramparts and towers, is one of the side-effects — and I suppose one of the benefits — of living in a part of the world that has not known war or even civil strife for almost two hundred years. But still, we are jealous of our boundaries. Back in New England they have a saying, "Good fences make good neighbours" — and by "fences," New Englanders mean stone walls, waist-high, always in good repair, and (above all) immoveable. The idea is not to wall your own livestock *in*, so much as to wall your neighbour's livestock *out*. There are those who see this as a reflection of the New England soul; but I am not so sure that building fences in order to wall others out as much as to wall yourself in, is peculiar to New Englanders alone. It is a human trait, a habit built into our nature; and though we no longer build walls around our cities, towns, and villages, we have invented invisible barriers to keep out people whom we do not know or do not like, and to protect certain parts of ourselves even from those we love.

A New England poet named Robert Frost once began a poem with this line: "Something there is that doesn't love a wall." In the present case, the something is a someone. God does not love a wall, or at least any wall that humans build that has the effect of shutting a creature out of — and off from —

the divine love. That is why God, when he wanted to show St. John an image of the new creation and the kingdom of heaven, gave him a vision of the new Jerusalem as an unwalled city, a city whose "gates will never be shut by day — and there will be no night there." And God is now at work building — or trying to build — that city on earth, even here among us. The Almighty is striving to make us realise that his own glory is the light of this community, and that our lamp, the lamp by which we read reality, is Christ the Lamb. If we can accept that, if we can open the eyes of our faith wide enough to see that this is so, then we shall have no cause for fear, nor any reason to wall ourselves in for the sake of walling others out.

The Sweet-Smelling Savour

When we celebrate the Ascension of our Lord Jesus Christ, we commemorate his going up in glory forty days after his resurrection. It is a happy feast — and an odd one. Odd, because it commemorates the Lord's going *up* — whereas almost every other festival celebrates God's coming *down*. At Christmas we rejoice that the Son of God leaped down out of heaven and took our flesh and dwelt among us; at Pentecost we commemorate the time when God sent down the Holy Spirit upon the apostles; in Advent we look forward to the day when the Lord will come down again in glory; and even in our ordinary feasts of the Lord, our Sunday eucharists, we pray the Father to send down his Word and Holy Spirit upon our oblation. But on Ascension Day, celebrating the going *up*, not the coming *down* of Jesus Christ.

Among all the feasts of our Lord, then, the feast of the Ascension appears to be the odd feast out. It is about an event that is, quite literally, out of this world; and, to be honest, St. Luke the evangelist, to whom alone we owe a circumstantial account of the event, does not altogether succeed in communicating the mystery of the moment. Luke says that Jesus "was lifted up, and a cloud took him out of [the apostles's] sight." The evangelist further reports that two angels appeared before the apostles to make the meaning of what had just happened perfectly clear: "This Jesus, who has been taken up from you into heaven, will come in the same way as you saw him go into heaven." So Jesus not only went up into a cloud; he entered "heaven" itself. And I have to confess that whenever I have read or heard these words, the first thing that has popped into my head is a line much loved by Trekkies: "Beam me up, Scotty. There's no intelligent life down here." No doubt the Ascension was a mighty wonder; but the miraculous mechanics of Luke's account get in the way of the meaning of the mystery, and its apparent violation of the laws of physics makes it hard to recognize the gospel, the good news, that the feast of the Ascension is meant to proclaim.

And what *is* the good news of the Ascension? It is not that God can spatially elevate bodies; no, the good news, the mystery, even the truth of the Ascension is that every other feast of the Lord — even Easter itself — is fulfilled in this feast of his going up in glory. For why did the Son of God descend from heaven and become a human being in the first place? It was for no other reason but to become our sacrifice — and the very fullness of all sacrifice, at that. For sacrifice is made so that our humanity may ascend into communion with God.

In ancient days, Israel was commanded to present animals from their flocks and herds, and the first-fruits of their crops, at the altars of God Most High. "The sons of the priest Aaron" were to "put fire on the altar, and arrange wood on the fire," and then roast the offering in the fire that it might become "a burnt offering, and offering by fire, of pleasing odour to the Lord" (Leviticus 1:7–8). The fire would mount up on the altar, and the flames would lick ever upward, and the sweet smell of the roasting meat would rise on the ascending smoke — would rise and rise and rise until its scent reached, as it were, the nostrils of the Almighty and delivered the people's invitation to their God, that the Almighty join them in their feast and become both their host and their guest in a communion of earth with heaven.

Such were the sacrifices of ancient Israel; and we say that Jesus offered sacrifice too — such a sacrifice as fulfilled all other kinds of sacrifice. Only, his altar was the cross and the fire of his sacrifice was love. For Christ's love burned toward the heart of heaven in a bright flame, until he was wholly consumed in it and went up in that fire to God. And that is his ascension: the Lord of creation came down from heaven to become our Passover, our paschal sacrifice — and by his sacrifice to kindle in us the living fire of love that tends always toward the heart of heaven. His humanity was not consumed but consummated by his sacrifice; and the human desire that once rose on the smoke of burnt offerings is now fulfilled through the ascension of his living love into the embrace of the Father in heaven.

And that same fire, the fire of Christ's love, is kindled on every altar of the Church, whenever Christians gather to offer their sacrifice of praise and thanksgiving, the eucharist. And there, on every altar of the Church, by Word and Spirit, Christ ascends in an unconsuming, unquenchable flame; there too, by bread and wine, the same fire is kindled in our hearts, and we ascend. For the Lord is in our midst, even within us, and says, "Lift up your hearts"; and we reply, "We lift them to the Lord!" Let us therefore be true to his sacrifice and on this feast of his ascension rise with the love that the partaking of his body and blood should set in our hearts; let us be faithful to his oblation, which here we share, that our love may be kindled and tend always upward, even to the very heart of God.

THE ETERNAL FUTURE

I have made your name known to those whom you gave me from the world. They were yours, and you gave them to me, and they have kept your word.... All mine are yours, and yours are mine; and I have been glorified in them. And now I am no longer in the world, but they are in the world, and I am coming to you. Holy Father, protect them in your name that you have given me, so that they may be one, as we are one.

(JOHN 17:6, 10–11)

Long, long ago, in a galaxy not all that far, far away from here, a certain young man underwent training as an ecclesiastical jedi at Trinity College, Toronto. He was not alone in this training program; for in those days there were many who aspired to be jedis for Jesus. Most of us were left to choose which jedi-knights we trained under; but certain mysteries of the ecclesiastical force we had to learn together, under a single master. One of these common learning-experiences was a required non-credit course in the mysteries of Anglican hymnody, as contained in the old Blue Hymn Book, *The Book of Common Praise, 1938.* The Obi-Wan Kenobi of this course was the Dean of Divinity himself, the Rev. Canon Howard W. Buchner; and as a consequence, we called the course Dean-Sing. Every Monday afternoon, between two and three o'clock, we second-year divinity students gathered in the choir loft of the college chapel, our copies of the Blue Hymnal before us, while the Dean, sitting at the organ console, led us through the whole book — hymn by hymn, tune by tune. We had pencils in our hands, ready to scribble down such comments as he deemed appropriate. Fr. Buchner had (and has still) very definite opinions about words and music, and he was not shy about expressing them with firm economy. A small canon of texts and tunes received the designation "Excellent"; the rest ranged from "All right," through "Dull" or "Not very good but you're stuck with it," to "NEVER!" The entire section entitled "Evangelistic Missions" came under the ban of "NEVER!"; but very few other hymns received this dire proscription. Indeed, the Dean rarely gave thumbs-down to a whole hymn; as a rule he blackballed only particular verses of a given hymn.

One such hymn was No. 263, "Christ is gone up," by that great confessor-saint of the Victorian Anglo-Catholic movement, John Mason Neale. It is the first of three hymns appointed for Ember Days and Ordination. The hymn has four verses, and Fr. Buchner had no trouble with the first, second, and fourth verses. Verse 3 was another matter. It reads:

So age by age, and year by year,
His grace was handed on;
And still the holy Church is here,
Although her Lord is gone.

In my own copy of the Blue Hymnal, this third verse is firmly crossed out in pencil — as sure a sign as the Dean ever gave, that the verse was heretical and NEVER to be sung. What Fr. Buchner objected to, as I remember, was Neale's suggestion that the Lord had left the Church more or less to its own devices, to administer a fixed supply of grace with which the Lord had endowed it before he went away. In proof that this view was wrong, Fr. Buchner even referred us to the final verse of the gospel according to Matthew, where the risen Lord tells his disciples, "And remember, I am with you always, to the end of the age" (Matthew 28:20B). It so happens that this same reference is picked up in today's Collect: we called upon the God who exalted Jesus Christ "with great triumph to the kingdom in heaven," then prayed that God would "give us faith to know that, as [Christ] promised, he abides with us on earth to the end of time." Christ is exalted, yes, but not gone — at least not in the sense implied by Neale's hymn.

And yet ... and yet, we have just celebrated the feast of the Ascension; and what is that feast about, if it is not about Christ's going up — and going away? So it seems that Jesus "don't get around much anymore," at least in the world as we know it. He is *not here* — or rather, *no longer* here — but somewhere else. Of course, that raises the question, *Where* has he gone? Where is he *now*? The Christian tradition has answered by pointing to the opening verses of the book of the Acts of the Apostles, which give a circumstantial account of the Ascension of the Lord. There it says that, on the fortieth day after the resurrection, "as [the disciples] were watching, [Jesus] was lifted up, and a cloud took him out of their sight. While he was going and they were gazing up toward heaven, suddenly two men in white robes stood by them. They said, 'Men of Galilee, why do you stand looking up toward heaven? This Jesus, who has been taken up from you into heaven, will come in the same way as you saw him go into heaven' " (Acts 1:9–11). So where has Jesus gone? The answer is easy: he has gone up into heaven.

The answer is easy; but I must confess that I do not find it helpful. In 1957 the Soviet Union sent its Sputnik satellite into orbit around the earth, the very first time that humans had succeeded in doing such a thing. Talk about getting "the first man into space" became the hot topic of the day, and somehow such a serious matter managed to percolate into the cartoon-soaked brain of a certain six-year-old. The idea of "a man in space" lodged itself in my brain as a speculative question, which went something like this: A rocket would send a man up into space; heaven is up in space; but you go to heaven only when you die. So what would happen to the spacemen when they entered heaven? I asked my mother this question, since she was the one who took my sister and me to church. My memory has not preserved her answer, but it could not have been very firm or even very encouraging, for soon afterwards we left the Roman Catholic Church and began attending the Unitarian-Universalist Society. Thus did I learn that religion is earnest and religion is real, and that thinking about heaven in particular can lead to big changes with serious consequences.

I also learned something else from that little episode in 1957. I learned to distrust any image of heaven as a place, as a somewhere "up there," or indeed anywhere at all. So for years after I returned to the Christian Church, my mind still felt embarrassed and uneasy whenever the feast of the Ascension rolled around — precisely because the account in the book of Acts, which supplies the rationale of the feast, states that Jesus has "gone into heaven," and simply takes it for granted that heaven must be a place, a somewhere "up there."

It is interesting to note by contrast that other writings in the New Testament, including the gospels according to Matthew, Mark, and John, are a good deal less specific — or a good deal more cagey — than Luke and the book of Acts, about what happened to Jesus after the resurrection. They have no interest in what might be called the mechanics of the ascension. The only point that really mattered to them was that Jesus came from and then went back to the Father — and so far as they were concerned, nothing more needed to be said. It would be going too far to say that these evangelists were agnostic about heaven; but they saw nothing to be gained from describing the mechanics of the mystery.

Which, when you come to think of it, is rather odd, because the other evangelists can hardly be said to have wimped out when it came to describing the disciples' encounters with the risen Jesus. So why stop at the ascension; why not go whole hog, as Luke did, and tell us how Jesus went to the kingdom in heaven? The explanation, or at least part of an explanation, may lie in the stories of the resurrection-appearances themselves. Anybody who reads them will be struck by the sense of awe that permeates the evangelists' accounts of the risen Lord; but with that sense of awe the several accounts also bear a certain discomfiture. It is not that the evangelists doubted the truth of what they were trying to recount. What disconcerted them was the very reality of that truth. Stories need to fit the dimensions of the space-time continuum, for such is the order of created reality that the human storytellers and their hearers inhabit. But each of the accounts of the resurrection in the New Testament is by a writer who knows that he is dealing with an event that no longer fits into space and time in any ordinary, straightforward, simple fashion. The resurrection certainly happened at a particular time, and in a particular place, but the New Testament accounts keep sending signals that the clock it followed ticked eternities instead of minutes, and that the place did not contain the risen Lord so much as his resurrection contained the place. In short, the ordinary rules of creation no longer apply; we are dealing with the rules of a creation made new.

And the problem that the evangelists have with pinning the risen Jesus down and making his resurrection fit the rules of the space-time continuum apply to his ascension too. For the ascension was the consummation of resurrection. But a consummation is not simply a continuation of the event it completes. It may involve such an intensity — the event may reach such a critical mass — that we can no longer speak of the event itself in the same terms. In this sense, then, the ascension of Christ may be viewed as the moment when the resurrection of Christ finally warped out of the present order of creation and became absolutely the new creation. Not only had Jesus "slipped the bonds of surly earth," he had also slipped the bonds of all language that is bound to the space-time continuum.

When we say that Jesus "ascended into heaven," therefore, we are not talking about *where* he now is so much as about *how* he now is. He now exists in the very godhood of God, immeasurably empowered with all of God's own life. And this is true of his humanity. The ascension not only represents the return of the co-eternal Word to his divine home, where he dwelt with the Father and the Spirit before the incarnation. The ascension of Jesus also represents the entry of our humanity into the very life of God, and our humanity's empowerment with all the glory, all the beauty of the Almighty. For Jesus ascended precisely as a human being, the new human being; and when his risen, newly created humanity entered into glory, our humanity went with him. Jesus is now what all of us will be — what all of us, by baptism and the eucharist, have been and are even now becoming. So his ascension is not about his going to a place "out beyond the shining / Of the farthest star." It is about his becoming our own eternal future.

And so it is that in John's gospel we hear Jesus pray to the One who sent him, saying: "Father, I desire that those also, whom you have given me, may be with me where I am.... I made your name known to them, and I will make it known, so that the love with which you have loved me may be in them, and I in them." And Jesus continued his prayer: "All mine are yours, and yours are mine; and I have been glorified in them. And now I am no longer in the world, but they are in the world, and I am coming to you. Holy Father, protect them in your name that you have given me, so that they may be one, as we are one." Not only are we with Christ where he is our eternal future; he is also with us where we are now. So then, wherever and whenever we gather, there the eternity that is Christ intersects with the present and converts that spot and that moment into a sacrament of the new creation.

And I will be so bold as to say that this is precisely the significance of each parish church and the community of which the building is the architectural sacrament. Our own parish community has been the intersection of time and eternity, of an ever-recurring present and the constant future that is Christ Jesus. Our life together is the space where Christ dwells in order to convert this moment, and every moment of our community's past, into the eternity of God's own life. And this building, this house of God, is the sacrament of that intersection and conversion. It, and you gathered within it, are the outward and visible sign of Immanuel, "God with us," precisely as our future, as all the fullness of what God always intended humans to become.

And that is why Fr. Neale did not speak the truth as he ought in his ordination hymn. It is precisely *because* Christ's holy Church is still here, that its Lord is not gone, but converting this and every present moment into his own eternity, where his new humanity and ours exists in perfect union with God the Word — and thus in constant communion with the Father and the Holy Spirit.

LIKE THE RUSH
OF A VIOLENT WIND

And suddenly from heaven there came a sound like the rush of a violent wind, and it filled the entire house where they were sitting.

(ACTS 2:2)

We Christians are caught in an awful bind — in a bind that is awful not just in the ordinary sense of something very unpleasant, but awful in the sense of being full of awe. Take the case at its most basic level. How do we pray? Or rather, as we pray, what reflexes of thought and feeling kick in concerning the God to whom we are praying? Scripture and the tradition of the Church have conditioned us to call upon God as the Almighty, the One who alone is all-powerful, who alone rules and even overrules everything that is. That is on one side; and it is (as I say) the indisputable witness of the Bible and the common prayer of the Church. But on the other side, there is the testimony of our own sentiments, garnered from places as diverse as Sunday School and ready-made greeting cards. And the witness of our sentiments tells us that, if God is almighty, God should also be *nice*. You know, polite, well-brought-up, full of innocent fun, and always smiling. The problem with this second witness is, it has no basis in Scripture or the prayer of the Church. Our religion certainly claims that God is omnipotent; but Christianity does not say that God must be *nice*. Indeed, on the whole, the Almighty is not *nice* at all.

Consider one of the most basic images that Scripture uses for the presence and action of God — the image of wind. The wind that the Scriptures imagine is not the steady light breeze that fills some canvas during a sunny afternoon's sail on a lake. On the contrary, it is the relentless, battering, brutalizing gales of a hurricane. And that is just the image that St. Luke used, when he imagined the descent of the Holy Spirit on that first day of Pentecost in Jerusalem: "And suddenly from heaven there came a sound like the rush of a violent wind, and it filled the entire house where they were sitting." Luke's comparison was not meant to suggest divine *niceness*; it was meant to reveal the Spirit's almighty power.

We are talking about raw power, sheer force, irresistable might. For that was Israel's elemental experience of the Lord their God. This God was known to them as much by the utter destruction he wreaked upon their enemies as by the marvels of salvation he wrought on their own behalf. And indeed, in much of the Old Testament, the power of God has nothing whatever to do with morality; it has to do with the insurmountable difference between mortals and the Almighty. Because of this difference, it is almost as if God could not help but destroy mortals who happened to trespass the borders of divinity; human notions of morality were irrelevant, because the Most High could not act in any other way and still be the Most High.

Such was Israel's experience of God; and this same experience informs the Church's own faith and practice. For we too address the very same God as the only sovereign and almighty power; and virtually all our collects turn on our appeal to the Father's mastery over all that is. There is elemental wisdom in such behaviour. After all, what is the point of worshipping a God that cannot do everything? And if the Almighty does not have the might to accomplish the impossible as a matter of course, why bother to pray at all? So, let us be frank: much of the Church's worship is focused on the raw power of God.

But there is another side to the worship of the Church, an aspect of the Almighty that is just as important but that we usually take for granted in our prayers. If we are creatures made to adore and obey the power of God, we are also beings created with a longing for meaning, with an ability to discern patterns behind and within the jumble of everyday life. And that is why we believe in God. For even as we acknowledge the might of the Almighty, and make our appeal to it, we also confess that God has a reason for acting, a meaning in mind, a goal in view. So when we pray, we not only appeal to limitless power; we appeal to One whose power is ever-ordained to a purpose. And the almighty purpose is always our salvation, never our destruction; God always seeks to convert our human lives, to make them capable of enjoying the three-personed existence of God's own divinity.

We come back to that upper room in Jerusalem on the day of Pentecost, to that moment when "there was a sound like the rush of a violent wind." The Holy Spirit was in that sound; and in that sound, the Spirit swept in upon those first disciples with all the might of the Almighty. Only, this time, the violence of the Spirit's descent did not wreak destruction. On the contrary, it worked salvation: it empowered those disciples to share in the power of the Almighty's purpose. They were sent out to proclaim "the wonderful works of God" to their own people, to the children of Israel, that they might know and believe in Jesus Christ, who was the fulfilment of God's promises to them and their forebears.

On that feast of Pentecost, then, the apostles received the power and gifts of the Spirit to carry out evangelism. Only, they were not sent out to evangelize unbelievers; they were sent out that morning to evangelize believers, the chosen people of God, their fellow Jews. When Peter spoke to the crowds of Jews who had gathered in Jerusalem from all parts of the Roman empire, his aim — or rather, the aim of the Spirit — was to build up the community of Israel. The Spirit rushed in upon the apostles so that they, being themselves empowered, might empower the holy people of God to share once for all in the power of the Almighty made manifest in the resurrection of his Son Jesus of Nazareth.

And to this very day, the same Spirit of holiness and power continues to rush in upon the Church for the same purpose — for the purpose of building up the community of God's people. True, we do not hear "a sound like the rush of a violent wind," nor is this house filled in any obvious way with the shattering power of the Spirit. The loudest sounds we hear are only those of the organ and our own voices joined in singing. Nevertheless, the Spirit is here, and breathes in the midst of this assembly, to empower us with the purpose of God, the building up of this community, yes, the building up of each other. Not private gifts or merely individual privileges for each one to enjoy separately; but gifts given so that each one might aid and abet the whole people of God in their enjoyment of God.

WIND AND FIRE

When the day of Pentecost had come, they were all together in one place. And suddenly from heaven there came a sound like the rush of a violent wind, and it filled the entire house where they were sitting. Divided tongues, as of fire, appeared among them, and a tongue rested on each of them. All of them were filled with the Holy Spirit.

(ACTS 2:1–4A)

We who live in Canada know that there are years of flame. Across the country, miles and miles and miles of forestland are consumed by fire, and whole towns have to evacuate before the storms of flame. These vast fires are the very definition of natural catastrophe, and the reports of the destruction they have wreaked only serve to confirm what we have always known, that fire is a terrible thing.

So it is somewhat strange to hear the story of the day of Pentecost — how the apostles "were all together in one place," when "suddenly from heaven there came a sound like the rush of a violent wind, and it filled the entire house where they were sitting. Divided tongues, as of fire, appeared among them, and a tongue rested on each of them. All of them were filled with the Holy Spirit." A lot of different things are packed into that story; but what might stick out for us in this springtime of woodland infernos is the fact that, after the mighty rushing wind had swept through the house where the apostles were gathered,

"Divided tongues, *as of fire*, appeared among them." Wind and fire — the two elements that the firefighters and people in northern Ontario, in Alberta, and in British Columbia have come to dread the most — these same elements are today the signs of God the Holy Spirit. Wind and fire, in combination, are the elements that engulf whole forests and threaten thriving towns with blazing destruction. And yet here, wind and fire signify the very opposite — not destruction but creation, not catastrophe but salvation, not the malevolent forces of nature but the blessing of the divine Spirit.

Of course, the wind and fire that St. Luke tells of — the wind that filled the whole house, and the tongues of flame that rested on each of the apostles — were also meant to be signs of power, divine power. And that may be why the Spirit chose these elements to make known its presence, precisely because wind and fire have such awesome power in nature. But the Spirit does something not only *with* but also *to* these elements. For the Spirit does more than simply use these forces of nature: it also changes them — you might even say, the Spirit converts wind and fire.

For what is it that make wind and fire so awesome — and so fearful — in nature? It is their very soullessness. They wreak destruction indiscriminately, and they spare without rhyme or reason; they make no choices, but hit everything in their path with the same force, and only other forces of nature, equally indifferent, equally soulless, can change that path. Yet here, on the day of Pentecost, wind and fire are no longer soulless, and no longer indiscriminate. The wind rushes into and fills only one house in all of Jerusalem; and the tongues of fire light on particular persons, not on all the city. What is more, like the bush that Moses saw in the wilderness, which was afire without being consumed, so the tongues of flame that rested on each of the disciples and the blessed Virgin Mary did not so much as singe them. Nature itself had been converted, to become a sacrament of the Holy Spirit.

Wind and fire, as signs and sacraments of the Spirit, remain powerful and very awesome; and as we have natural sense enough not to play with fire, so we should have the sense of faith not to fool around with the Spirit. As the forces of nature can be dangerous, so can the Spirit be. And yet, as was pointed out by several experts when the forest fires in the west were at their worst, such conflagrations are often for the benefit of the very forests they consume. Fire cleanses the woodland, clears the forest of deadwood and choking undergrowth, and makes possible new growth. Just so with the fire of the Spirit. For the Spirit came down as on this day, and abides even yet in the community of the Church, to make new growth possible; and as the Spirit of God swept over the face of chaos at the beginning of creation, in order that God might speak the Word that makes things be, so does the Spirit brood over this church, and over each one of us, that God the Source of all being might speak the Word, the Word made flesh, who is Jesus, into our very lives and make us the new creation — each of us set aflame, to set the world on fire with the love of God that is in Christ Jesus our Lord.

Codas

EQUIPPING THE SAINTS

The gifts he gave were that some would be apostles, some prophets, some evangelists, some pastors and teachers, to equip the saints for the work of ministry, for building up the body of Christ, until all of us come to the unity of the faith and of the knowledge of the Son of God, to maturity, to the measure of the full stature of Christ.

(EPHESIANS 4:11–13)

Once upon a time, in the grand city of St. John's, New foundland, there was a certain curate on the staff of the Anglican cathedral. The staff was not very large; in fact, this curate was the only other full-time priest, besides the Dean. Which meant that this curate found himself kept very busy indeed, with a wide variety of duties — visits to parishioners in their homes, visits to parishioners in one or another of the hospitals, conducting tours of the cathedral for school-children, preparing Sunday sermons, drafting rotas of servers, supervising Sunday school, teaching confirmation classes, answering the phone, and answering the phone, and answering the phone…. But each day opened and closed in the same way — with Morning Prayer at seven a.m., followed by the eucharist, and with Evening Prayer every night at five-thirty. The curate had one day off every week, but only after he had done Mattins and eucharist, and only until it was time for Evensong. Since the curate was there to keep the prayer-wheel going, the Dean saw no reason to interrupt his own days off by attending the services. After all, what are curates for, if not to afford their elders and betters the liberty of a dignified ease?

And so it happened one evening in early spring, that the curate emerged from the cathedral alone, having just said Evensong alone in the cathedral's Lady chapel. Now, if you have ever visited St. John's in April, you will know that on the Rock, "spring" is a relative term. Newfoundland has only two seasons — summer and fog; and the season of fog runs from the end of September to the second week of August. So that particular evening, though the sun was shining as the curate locked the cathedral doors, he was dressed against the chill of a North Atlantic winter. And that meant a very particular outfit, for the Dean insisted on proper clerical attire. No parkas and woolly toques, but black cassock, black sweater, black scarf, a heavy, ankle-length black cape, and to crown it all, a black biretta — one of those funny hats that make a priest look like Mickey Mouse with a pom-pom and one ear missing.

Thus dressed, the curate locked the side door of the cathedral, and crossed the street on his way back to the clergy house. He stepped on to the opposite sidewalk, and encountered a woman with two girls, both around nine or ten years old. As they passed the curate, one of the girls said, "Ev'nin', Rev'rend!" The curate nodded his head in a priestly manner, and moved on. He had taken only two or three steps, when he heard the other girl whisper fiercely to the one who had greeted him, "That's not a Rev'rend, stupid, that's a *Father!*" It made my whole day.

I do not know whether Canon Sheen — Susan — will require Naomi henceforth to wear distinctive priestly garb while going about her parish duties; I suspect not. But it is important to remember that, whatever Naomi wears, she's not a Rev'rend

— she's a Mother. That is to say, a mother of the churches in this parish, an elder who is here to nurture the children of God in Millbrook, Baillieboro, the Marsh, Bethany, and Lifford. And as good mothers nurture their children, not to keep them children, but to help them grow up and become adults, so Naomi will be in your midst as a mother of the Church, not to keep you down, but (as St. Paul says in this evening's epistle) "to equip the saints" — to equip *you* — "for the work of ministry, for building up the body of Christ, until all of us come to the unity of the faith and of the knowledge of the Son of God, to maturity, to the measure of the full stature of Christ." Tonight Naomi is to become a priest for your sake, and for the sake of the whole Church, to help us children of God all grow "to maturity" as sharers in the life of his Son Jesus Christ.

To be sure, Naomi is a young woman; and the fact of her youth might seem to be at odds with viewing her not only as a mother of the Church but also as a priest. For the word *priest* is derived from the Greek word for "elder." How can a person so much younger than many of you be your elder, with all the authority that an elder is supposed to have?

By way of an answer, the first thing to say is that priests are made, not born. Nobody comes to the priesthood ready-made or already stocked with the authority that belongs to the order. Some priests may have natural charisma, what might be called animal magnetism, before they are ordained; and the rest of us poor mortals are prone to think that this constitutes their suitability for priesthood, and the only charter of authority that we need to see. Such charisma or animal magnetism may lubricate their ministry and make it easier for them to get their way. But it is not the same as the authority of the ministerial priesthood, nor is that authority theirs — or any other priest's — by right. For, as I say, priests are made, and what authority they have is given to them through ordination by a bishop, acting on behalf of the whole community of the Church. Indeed, as priests hold their orders from their bishop, so do they derive their authority from their bishop. Priests are, first and foremost, representatives of the bishop; and as the bishop is the eye through which the unity of the Church is threaded, to bind his or her diocese to the one communion and fellowship of God's people throughout the earth, so is a priest the eye through which the bishop's authority is threaded to bind any one parish and local community both to the diocese and, beyond, to the worldwide communion of the Church. In the first place, then, a priest serves a parish or community by connecting its people with their bishop and thus, as the bishop's representative, connecting the parish with the universal Church. That is the office of priest, and that is the only warrant of a priest's authority.

And if the priest's authority is to represent the bishop in communion with the whole Church, it follows that the priest's age in years has nothing to do with the priest's eldership in the community. For the Church is a community of gifts — what do we have that we did not receive as a gift from God (1 Corinthians 4:7B)? — and it may be that the Holy Spirit has gifted one or another person — may have gifted Naomi — with a particular variety of ministry for the sake of enabling the gifts that the Spirit has bestowed on others in this parish and in the wider Church. One does not have to be great in years to be great in gifts, or even in one particular gift, so long as the gift given to the priest is then given by the priest to those whom she has been sent to serve.

And I say to you all, even as I say it to Naomi on this her priesting day: Do not expect the variety of ministry with which Naomi has been gifted to be always and at every turn brilliantly obvious. The Church is not ordaining Naomi to be a celebrity;

we are ordaining her to be a priest. And much, if not most, of a priest's life and service is hidden — hidden out in the open. I know, I know — "No one after lighting a lamp puts it under the bushel basket, but on the lampstand, and it gives light to all in the house" (Matthew 5:15). The lamp itself might be a beautiful piece of furniture, but we do not put it on the lampstand in order that the thing itself may be seen and looked at; we put it there in order that it may allow us to see and look at and work on other things by the light it gives. Just so with priests: the Church ordains them, bestows authority on them, and puts them up front, not in order that they may be admired for themselves, but in order that they may give us the kind of light by which we may see our own callings the better and act on them the more truly.

This is what St. Paul meant when he said that Christ calls and gifts some individuals to be priests "to equip the saints for the work of ministry." So Naomi has been called and will be gifted tonight with the authority of a priest — not to smother you but to mother you; not to rule over you but to equip you in such a way that you, and every other member of the Church to whom she will be a priest, may lay hold of the gifts that the Spirit has given to you and serve each other as members and sharers of the body of Christ.

DIVERSIFIED UNITY

In the year that King Uzziah died, I saw the Lord sitting on a throne, high and lofty; and the hem of his robe filled the temple. Seraphs were in attendance above him; each had six wings: with two they covered their faces, and with two they covered their feet, and with two they flew. And one called to another and said:

"Holy, holy, holy is the Lord of hosts;
the whole earth is full of his glory."

... Then I heard the voice of the Lord saying, "Whom shall I send, and who will go for us?" And I said, "Here am I; send me!"

(ISAIAH 6:1–3, 8)

When we cry, "Abba! Father!" it is [the Holy] Spirit bearing witness with our spirit that we are children of God, and if children, then heirs, heirs of God and joint heirs with Christ.

(ROMANS 8:15–17)

In a parish with a staff of several priests, Trinity Sunday is like the famous advertisement for a certain breakfast cereal. You may remember the ad: Two boys are sitting at the table squinting at a box they have never seen before. One says to the other, "Are *you* going to try it?" The other says, "*I'm* not going to try it." A beat passes, as they continue to give the new box the hairy eyeball. Then the first boy has an inspiration. "I know — let's give it to Mikey. He hates everything." Cut to a three- or four-year old whose pudgy face is the very incarnation of bad attitude. But it turns out that Mikey likes the cereal; the last scene of the ad shows him gleefully shoveling spoonfuls of the stuff into his mouth. The resemblance of the ad to Trinity Sunday ends there. In a parish with a staff of (say) three priests, we should imagine two of them staring glumly at a draft of the preaching rota. The first says, "Are you going to preach on Trinity Sunday?" The second says, "*I'm* not going to preach on Trinity Sunday." A beat passes, then the first priest says, "I know — let's give it to the Theologian in Residence. He's *supposed* to know all about the Trinity!"

I cannot say that anything like this conversation took place in the Incumbent's office, between herself and the Associate Priest. But, imaginary though it may be, the conversation is true in spirit. For this is the one Sunday that most preachers dread, because it is the Sunday when preachers have to do — God save us! — THEOLOGY. It is certainly not the case with the clergy of this parish, but a great many clergy harboured a fear of theology before they entered divinity school, and have nursed a resentment of it ever since, as something that gets in the way of the "real" needs of the Church. But then, in a book published just this month, Gary Wills has offered us poor, pointy-headed theologians a small measure of vindication. Wills is not only one of the most wide-ranging American intellectuals writing today; he is also a practising Roman Catholic, who attends mass at least weekly. Early on in his new book, he writes of the frustration felt by many lay people like himself. Sitting in the pew of his parish church on a certain Sunday after Pentecost, he noted how "[a] priest was almost apologetic when he had to refer to the Trinity, 'a rather abstruse matter,' just because it was Trinity Sunday." Wills then commented: "I wondered what he thought we were there to hear about if the central doctrines of the faith were irrelevant."[1] Good point. So then, since it is Trinity Sunday, what *is* the doctrine of the Trinity? It is simply this: that God, the only God, is one being and three persons. "Simply," he says! That is where the preacher that Gary Wills heard, like so many other preachers, shrank before the challenge and apologized for the abstruseness of the truth. The Anglican Church once required its members to say, on certain designated Sundays and festivals, the confession of faith known as the Athanasian Creed — the creed that begins, "Whosoever would be saved needeth before all things to hold fast the Catholic Faith. Which Faith except a man keep whole and undefiled, without doubt we will perish eternally." I personally think it is great stuff, a kind of confessional mantra for Christians. But the old Prayer Book translation gave rise to some unedifying mirth when in the ninth and twelfth verses it had us confess: "The Father is incomprehensible, the Son is incomprehensible, and the Holy Ghost is incomprehensible.... And yet there are not ... three incomprehensibles, but ... one incomprehensible." Many Christians would respond, "That is for sure!" For how can a single reality be both one and three? Talk about incomprehensible!

The Latin word that the old version of the Athanasian Creed rendered as "incomprehensible" was *immensus* — which actually means "unlimited" or "immeasurable," something that cannot be caught, caged, and confined in a religious zoo or a

---

1. Gary Wills, *Papal Sin: Structures of Deceit* (New York: Doubleday, 2000), p. 3.

human formula. It is that very acknowledgement that makes the Athanasian Creed such good stuff: it reminds us that the reality of the God we confess, worship, adore, and love cannot be exhausted by our thought, or domesticated by our quotidian needs. This God remains sovereign in mystery as in mercy.

But it is precisely the mercy of God to make the mystery of God known to us — and known to us precisely as mystery, the *immensus*, unlimited, immeasurable, inexhaustible mystery. Such is the message of Isaiah's vision in this morning's first reading. "In the year that King Uzziah died," the prophet "saw the Lord sitting on a throne, high and lofty; and the hem of his robe filled the temple. Seraphs were in attendance above him; each had six wings: with two they covered their faces, and with two they covered their feet, and with two they flew." Seraphim are an order of angels, by definition creatures of utmost purity; and yet even the seraphim must cover their faces in the presence of God. So holy is the glory of the Almighty, that not even they cannot look upon the One whom they acclaim. Thomas Aquinas said that angels are pure intelligences; and perhaps we may add that their intelligence is in their awe before the God they serve — or rather, that their awe *is* their intelligence. It is smart to be daunted by the Holy One.

And that is precisely what causes the prophet to break down: he is appalled by the vision, because he, "a man of unclean lips, [living] among a people of unclean lips," beholds what the seraphim dare not look at. So the vision not only reveals the immense glory of "the King, the Lord of hosts"; it also reveals the terrific immensity of the gap between the glory of the Lord and mere mortals. But that is not the end of the vision. For it is precisely at that point, at the moment of Isaiah's total self-abasement, that the Lord sends a seraph to heal him, to purify him, and to make him capable of bearing and speaking the Lord's own word to the people. The utter mystery that is God makes it possible for a human being to utter the selfsame mystery in human language.

Now, in the world of Isaiah's vision, it is none of the prophet's call to speculate on the inner life of God; the prophet is simply empowered to proclaim God's word, which is God's will and therefore what God *does*. For the witness of Isaiah, as of the other prophets in the Scriptures, is that God's will, God's word, and God's action are seamless; there is no gap or time-and-space-lapse between God willing something to happen, saying that it will happen, and its happening: "For [the Lord] spoke, and it came to be; [God] commanded, and it stood firm" (Psalm 33:9). But here we come upon a dimension of the prophet's call that is never fully articulated in the Scriptures but is always assumed. God's will-word-action is ordained to the covenant that God has made with the children of Israel. Which is to say: God speaks a word that enacts God's faithfulness to the conditions of the divine relationship with the people, even when the people have been faithless to those conditions. The prophet is specifically called to bear witness to God's fidelity. And that means, the prophet is empowered to discern and proclaim the *pattern* of God's action in the world. For without pattern there is no meaning in the actions; and without meaning there can be no reason for faithfulness *on our part*, except terror. Perhaps that is the deeper message of Isaiah in recounting his vision. His first reaction is fear; his final reaction is responsibility: "Then I heard the voice of the Lord saying, 'Whom shall I send, and who will go for us?' And I said, 'Here am I; send me!'" The mystery that is God does not seek to terrorize us into submission; the mystery that is God seeks to make us partners in a mutual relationship, in a pattern of mutual responsibility.

It is precisely the pattern of divine action, and the Church's experience of it, that has given rise to the doctrine of the Trinity. We see this in St. Paul's Letter to the Romans. The apostle proclaims a pattern that is also an experience. He says: "When we cry, 'Abba! Father!' it is [the Holy] Spirit bearing witness with our spirit that we are children of God, and if children, then heirs, heirs of God and joint heirs with Christ." The Holy Spirit acts in us to call upon God as "Abba," and the same Spirit reminds us that it is our baptism into Christ that enables us to do so: God is our "Abba" because we know that Christ, the only child of the "Abba," is our life. Abba, Christ, and Spirit — Spirit, Abba, and Christ — there is a triadic pattern in God's action; and this triadic pattern is not a set of three things, or three ideas, or three attributes, but the action of three *persons*. And because God is faithful to the way God *acts*, the triadic pattern is true to the way that God *is*. God is one, but God is also the mutual relationship of three persons in a pattern of mutual responsibility.

How we keep those two affirmations together — that God is one being and God is three persons — forms the stuff of Christian history and Christian spirituality; as well as of Christian theology. And I am here to tell you that there is no one single and simple fix-it answer. For the three-personed God remains sovereign in mystery as in mercy. And yet, mystery is an invitation to ceaseless exploration, not a permission-slip for ignorance; and even as we acknowledge that we shall never, ever know all there is about God, we also confess that God has given us not only enough to start with, but also plenty enough to keep us supplied as we journey toward (and into) the divine life. After all, "not knowing everything is not the same as knowing nothing."[2]

Legend has it that St. Patrick taught the Irish to believe the doctrine of the Trinity by holding up a shamrock — a single clover with three leafs. Okay; the triune God is like a shamrock. But where do we go from there — especially if we remember that it is looking over a *four*-leafed clover that is supposed to be lucky? I have heard and seen at least two preachers try to explain the triune mystery of God by taking an apple and slicing it three ways; Okay — except for the fact that we ended up with three separate pieces, not one apple. So perhaps we should stop looking for images in the vegetable order and turn to the image of God that the Scriptures identify as such. That is, we should turn and look at one another face to face. For it is our very diversity as a community — as a community in communion — that makes us the image and likeness of God.

To be sure, we are at times only too well aware of our diversity; it is the unity of our humanity that we have trouble realizing, and so routinely fail to realize. Perhaps that is because, as a race of creatures, we start out *being* diverse; unity is something we are called to achieve, not something we own by nature. And when it is achieved, it will always be the coming together of different individuals — as it were, a unified diversity. But God from all eternity is a diversified unity. That is to say, the unity of God is never without the diversity of the three persons; and the diversity of the three persons is always within the unity of a single life. Imagine a pattern of relationship in

---

2. Gerald O'Collins, *Fundamental Theology*.

which each partner not only shares all that he or she has with the others but also lives into the others, to establish each of the others in all their fullness. Now, that is not just a pattern of relationship; that is *communion*. God, the three-personed God, was, and is, and ever shall be what we strive to enact this morning around and at this altar — a communion of life mutually shared, where diversity is not swallowed up but truly fulfilled in unity.

THE DIVINE POLYPHONY

*Therefore, since we are justified by faith, we have peace with
God through our Lord Jesus Christ, through whom we have
obtained access to this grace in which we stand; and we boast
in our hope of sharing the glory of God.*

(ROMANS 5:1–2)

In the late spring of 1944 a young Lutheran theologian
named Dietrich Bonhoeffer sat in a prison just outside Berlin. The Gestapo had arrested him a year earlier because many
of his contacts and several of his trips had aroused its agents'
suspicions. Though being a prisoner of the Nazi State could be
very grim indeed, Bonhoeffer's confinement was not especially
harsh — at least, not yet. He could still receive letters and packages from his family and friends; he was free to read what books
he liked, and to send regular letters to his parents, his fiancée,
and a small circle of comrades. In fact, the only real discomfort
that Bonhoeffer experienced during this time as a prisoner of
the Third Reich came from the air raid alerts, as Allied bombers pummelled Berlin by day and by night. In the aftermath of
one such raid in May 1944, he made an observation, and jotted
it down in a letter to a former student, then serving on the
Russian front. Bonhoeffer wrote: "I notice repeatedly here how
few people there are who can harbour conflicting emotions at
the same time. When bombers come, they are all fear; when
there is something nice to eat, they are all greed; when they are
disappointed, they are all despair; when they are successful, they

can think of nothing else. They miss the fullness of life and the wholeness of an independent existence; everything objective and subjective is dissolved for them into fragments." Bonhoeffer was reflecting on prison life, or rather on the life of prisoners; but he clearly thought that his observation applied to those on the outside too, and to modern life in general. It is a characteristic of the modern world — in Canada today, as well as in the embattled Third Reich then — that people "miss the fullness of life" and let it be "dissolved for them into fragments." Such an observation was hardly original, or even especially Christian; secularist thinkers of the time had made similar observations. But Bonhoeffer was a Christian theologian, and his faith extended his observation into an insight. His letter continued: "By contrast, Christianity puts us into many different dimensions of life at the same time; we make room in ourselves, to some extent, for God and the whole world.... When the [air raid] alert goes, for instance: as soon as we turn our minds from worrying about our own safety to the task of helping other people to keep calm, the situation is completely changed; life isn't pushed back into a single dimension, but is kept multi-dimensional and polyphonous.... We have to get people out of their one-track minds; that is ... something that makes faith possible, although really it's only faith itself that can make possible a multi-dimensional life...." [1]

Living "a multi-dimensional life"... Bonhoeffer also spoke of keeping life "polyphonous." Polyphony is something we hear — and some of us even get to sing — quite regularly in this community. It is, quite literally, many sounds — a variety of

---

1. Dietrich Bonhoeffer, *Letters and Papers from Prison*, pp. 310–312 (29 May 1944).

voices singing in consort, in such a way that their variety is heard as a unity; indeed, in such a way that their variety *is* their unity. For unity is not the same as uniformity. Uniformity is the quashing of variety and diversity, so that all voices make the same sound. Unity, on the contrary, presumes diversity and variety, and so is a matter of combining distinct voices in mutual relation to one another in order to enrich the music. Hearing the polyphony of creation, attending to the unity of the many and various voices of our own humanity, remains no less a challenge for us today, than it was for Dietrich Bonhoeffer in May 1944. But, as Bonhoeffer went on to suggest, it is a challenge that Christians, when they are faithful and truest to their own truth, are well placed to meet.

What makes Christianity so well placed to meet the challenge of hearing the polyphony of existence is a reason that Bonhoeffer himself did not think to mention. It is the very truth, the very mystery, that we celebrate on this Sunday — the truth that God is the most Holy Trinity, that the persons we call the Father, the Son, and the Holy Spirit, are the one God, living and true. Think of the Trinity as if it were divine polyphony, a consort so united in their variegated expression of the one divine nature that the diversity of the three voices, the three persons, *is* the divine unity. There is no divine nature prior to, apart from, or after the persons. The mutual interrelation of the persons is how the divine nature exists; the one divine nature is the song that this three-personed polyphony sings, and sings eternally.

It is odd, I know, to liken the Trinity to a consort of music. Our tradition is far more accustomed to think that song belongs to creatures. Horatio desired that "choirs of angels waft" Hamlet "to his rest"; and when we come to celebrate the Church's great thanksgiving, we ourselves consort with angels and archangels and all the company of heaven to sing the threefold Holy of the seraphim. Our ancestors looked into the night sky and spoke of the music of the spheres; and we today still delight to sing hymns, and psalms, and spiritual songs. So, if the tradition is anything to go by, polyphony is something that creation and creatures sing *to* God — not something that the Father, the Son, and the Holy Spirit sing each to each, not something that God *is*.

But entertain — or endure — my conceit for a while longer. If angels and archangels can give no higher praise to the God who created them, than to *sing* that praise, where did they get the power to do so? If the spheres of the cosmos make music in their courses, who gave them the capacity to hum their melody? And if birds sing, if dolphins and whales ever-make a joyful noise, if humans sing out hymns and songs to magnify the God who made all things, where did the power of music, and the grace to practise it, come from? From where and from whom else but God the most holy Trinity? For, as God is the source of all being, who has imparted life to creation and all the diversity of creatures, so is God's own life the source of all music in the cosmos, and the only composer who seeks to bring the polyphony of creatures into unity with the polyphony that is the Father, the Son, and the Holy Spirit singing the divine nature in, and with, and through each other.

In today's reading from the Letter to the Romans, the Apostle said: "We boast in our hope of sharing the glory of God." Perhaps what I have said is a way of imagining what it means to share the glory of God. We share that glory so far as we learn and teach each other the polyphony that entertains diversity precisely as the premise of unity, and unity precisely as the sustenance of diversity. For that is God's gift of song to us and to all creation; it is the grace that is a kind of beginning of glory in us, because then we have begun to audition for the consort of the Trinity. And if we tune our lives and relations with one another to the melody of God, there can be no fear of failing the trial. For none is so faithful and true as the three Persons in welcoming voices into the consort and communion of the one polyphonous life of divinity.

ABC Publishing
ANGLICAN BOOK CENTRE

The Faithful Servant Series Christopher L. Webber, Series Editor. Thoughtful meditations on the rich and varied experience of volunteering in the church. Written by lay people for lay people. Each meditation is based on the words of scripture, liturgy, or hymn. Excellent gifts or company for any season. The series includes *Meditations for* ...

Altar Guild Members 0-8192-1845-6
Choir Members 0-8192-1779-4
Church School Teachers 0-8192-1861-8
Church Staff 0-8192-1919-3
Lay Eucharistic Ministers 0-8192-1770-0
Lay Readers 0-8192-1771-9
New Members 0-8192-1821-9
Vestry Members 0-8192-1789-1
$9.95 each

The Word Today: Reflections on the Readings of the Revised Common Lectionary by Herbert O'Driscoll. Continually fresh and varied, these reflections on the three readings and psalm for each Sunday of the Christian year take us deeply into scripture and, at the same time, deeply into our own life and time.

Year A1 1-55126-331-9 $14.95
Year A2 1-55126-332-7 $14.95
Year A3 1-55126-333-5 $18.95
Year B1 1-55126-334-3 $14.95
Year B2 1-55126-335-1 $14.95
Year B3 1-55126-336-X $18.95
Year C1 1-55126-337-8 $14.95
Year C2 1-55126-338-6 $14.95
Year C3 1-55126-339-4 $18.95

Visit our website: www.abcpublishing.com
Available from your local bookstore or Anglican Book Centre, phone 1-800-268-1168 or write 600 Jarvis St., Toronto, ON M4Y 2J6

Path Books
A LIGHT TO MY PATH

Practical spirituality to enrich everyday living

Practical Prayer: Making Space for God in Everyday Life by Anne Tanner. A richly textured presentation of the history, practices, and implications of Christian prayer and meditation to help people live a rewarding life in a stressful world.
1-55126-321-1 $18.95

Meditation CD: 1-55126-348-3 $18.95
Audio cassette: 1-55126-349-1 $16.95
Leader's Guide: 1-55126-347-5 $18.95

Prayer Companion: A Treasury of Personal Meditation by Judith Lawrence. A personal prayer resource providing gems for daily living, meditation, and prayer. A friendly companion to those searching for greater meaning in everyday experience.
1-55126-319-X $18.95

The Habit of Hope: In a Changing and Uncertain World by William Hockin. Wise and friendly guidance to help people living in an age of confusion and change to transform personal experience in the light of biblical story.
1-55126-325-4 $14.95

Passiontide: A Novel by Brian Pearson. In the midst of a spirited West Coast people, David, an Anglican priest, veers into the tangled realms of love and passion, and stares even into the jaws of death. This unpredictable pilgrimage of the soul makes no guarantees and offers no safe haven. He will never be the same again.
1-55126-350-5 $24.95

From Fear to Freedom: Abused Wives Find Hope and Healing by Sheila A. Rogers. This book recounts the spiritual journey of five women as they move from childhood into abusive marriages, and then out into self-realization and freedom. The women share their thoughts and feelings about themselves, their abusers, and God. The book offers practical advice for those who have experienced abuse, and for their friends and family.
1-55125-358-0 $19.95

God with Us: The Companionship of Jesus in the Challenges of Life by Herbert O'Driscoll. In thirty-three perceptive meditations, Herbert O'Driscoll considers the challenges of being human, searches key events in the life of Jesus, and discovers new vitality and guidance for our living. He shows how the healing wisdom and power of Jesus' life can transform our own lives today.
1-55126-359-9 $18.95

Path Books is an imprint of ABC Publishing. Please visit our website at *www.pathbooks.com*.